James Henry Stark

Illustrated History of Boston Harbor

James Henry Stark

Illustrated History of Boston Harbor

ISBN/EAN: 9783744733359

Printed in Europe, USA, Canada, Australia, Japan

Cover: Foto ©ninafisch / pixelio.de

More available books at **www.hansebooks.com**

ILLUSTRATED HISTORY

OF

BOSTON HARBOR

COMPILED FROM THE MOST AUTHENTIC SOURCES, GIVING A COMPLETE
AND RELIABLE HISTORY OF EVERY ISLAND AND HEAD-
LAND IN THE HARBOR, FROM THE EARLIEST
DATE TO THE PRESENT TIME.

Profusely Illustrated, and containing a Correct Map of the Harbor.

BY JAMES H. STARK.

BOSTON:
PUBLISHED BY THE PHOTO-ELECTROTYPE COMPANY,
171 DEVONSHIRE STREET.
1880.

PREFACE.

The compiler of this small history of Boston Harbor and its Islands has endeavored to give a correct and faithful account of it. The information contained therein is collected from the most authentic sources, and can be relied on as being strictly correct and not embellished or exaggerated in the least. It is compiled from such authorities as Snow's, Drake's, and Shurtleff's Histories of Boston, and from matter collected from the records in the possession of the New-England Historic, Genealogical Society.

The author has spent all his leisure time, since he was old enough to handle the tiller, in yachting in our beautiful harbor; and cruising along the adjacent coast. Not a week passes in the summer season but that at least a day is spent down the harbor. During these trips much of the matter in this work has been collected that came under the author's own personal observation; and, if it proves interesting to the reader, he will feel amply compensated for the time and trouble spent in this undertaking.

ILLUSTRATED HISTORY

OF

BOSTON HARBOR.

INTRODUCTION.

It is a strange fact, but nevertheless true, that, of the thousands of people in Boston, many have never been down the harbor, and but very few indeed can give an intelligent answer to queries from strangers relating to their beautiful island-dotted harbor. This may be accounted for, from the fact, that, until quite recently, only one line of steamers stopping at Hull and Hingham was employed for carrying passengers. Previous to this, the only way to reach these places was by a few old fishing boats at Long Wharf that could be hired, and a few yachts owned by private parties.

Within the past few years, a wonderful change has taken place. Many beautiful steamboats traverse the harbor in every direction, touching at the principal islands and beaches, and carrying crowds of pleasure-seekers every pleasant day. Places that a short time since showed no more signs of human habitation than the coast of Labrador, and seemingly as forsaken as when the white man first put his foot upon these shores, are now dotted with villas and hotels, and frequented during the summer months by thousands of visitors.

During the past few years, the number of cottages, many of them almost palatial in their appointments, have rapidly increased.

MAMMOTH HOTELS AND PAVILIONS

have sprung up almost by magic, until the shore stretching away on either hand, might be mistaken for one of those beautiful Oriental Cities. This illusion is the more striking from the prevailing Eastern style of architecture, and the dark-red covering that forms an important feature in the outer ornamentation of hundreds of structures.

The time-honored, chaste, and beautiful white cottages with green blinds, have given place to parti-colored effects, in which drabs and brown predominate below, while the upper portion is red and black.

The great popularity that our sea-shore resorts enjoy is found for one reason in the superb steamboat accommodations, which are said by travelers to be unequaled. They are models of strength, speed, and beauty, noted for their cleanliness and comfort, each and every owner and officer vying with each other to offer to their patrons the neatest and best-appointed pleasure steamer in the country.

THE HARBOR,

with its wide expanse of smooth water, its scores of picturesque islands, and its countless objects of interest, many of them rich in historic incidents, forms an unceasing and alluring attraction, not alone to the residents of our city and state, but to thousands of tourists, in whose estimation Boston's sea-shore attractions are unsurpassed in the country.

In the wide range of charming resorts, at which days and weeks may be spent with unabated enjoyment, lies the secret of the world-wide popularity of *Boston Harbor*.

On this coast, there is none that will equal it, in its picturesque effects. Its entrance is protected by the

ROCK-BOUND BREWSTERS

that break the ocean's swell, which continually thunders against its rocky barriers. Once inside its harbor, and it is as smooth as an inland lake, and much less liable to sudden squalls and flaws of wind; its waters are broad and deep, studded with numerous islands, which afford excellent camping-ground for the summer excursionists, who for weeks at a time enjoy themselves in fishing, gunning, yachting, bathing, and worshiping nature in all its beauty. For yachting purposes, it is certainly unequaled anywhere. A portion of its broad water the yachtmen have all to themselves, and are not troubled with steamers, vessels, scows, and so forth, which is usually the case in all waters near large cities, the vessels passing in and out of the harbor confining themselves generally to the main ship-channel.

YACHTING

has also increased in the last few years, and now several yacht clubs are organized with hundreds of sail. They are to be seen in every direction on a fine day, presenting a beautiful appearance, with their snowy sails and graceful models. There is now but one thing wanted, and that is, a suitable hand-book of information, at a price within every one's means, that will give an accurate description of the harbor and islands, and all necessary information, together with suitable illustrations of the principal objects to be seen in a day's trip. In this little volume we will endeavor to meet this want, and state also the best routes to take, to enjoy

A DAY DOWN THE HARBOR,

where it can be spent to the best advantage, also the best places to camp, and to enjoy yachting, gunning, fishing, and so forth, where the

BEST HOTELS

are located, and how reached, what their facilities are, prices, etc.

We will also lay out several excursion routes, giving a description of everything seen on the way, illustrating the principal points of interest by finely executed engravings, from photographs and sketches, together with a map of the harbor accurately projected from charts of the United States Coast Survey, and which shows the harbor and islands, as they would appear from a lofty eminence, in such a manner that the reader can readily see and understand the form of the harbor, islands and projecting points of the main land. The illustrations and map were made by the PHOTO-ELECTROTYPE ENGRAVING AND MANUFACTURING COMPANY, of Boston, who are the publishers of this hand-book of information for summer pleasure-seekers in Boston Harbor.

CHAPTER I.

EXCURSION NO. I FROM ROWE'S WHARF TO NANTASKET BEACH. — FORT POINT, AND THE OLD SCONCE BATTERY. — CHARLESTOWN, BUNKER-HILL MONUMENT, AND NAVY YARD. — DESCRIPTION OF EAST BOSTON, FORMERLY CALLED NODDLE'S ISLAND. — SOUTH BOSTON, FORMERLY CALLED MATTAPANNOCK. — WASHINGTON AT DORCHESTER HEIGHTS. — THE BRITISH ARE COMPELLED TO EVACUATE BOSTON.

Having given a slight account of the points of interest in Boston Harbor, we will now endeavor to describe the harbor, its islands, roads, channels, rocks, and spits. Instead of parading them in a tabular statement, in an alphabetical order, the plan will be pursued of laying out several routes to take to enjoy a day down the harbor, describing the various objects that may be seen on a day's excursion.

EXCURSION NO. I.

From Rowe's Wharf on Atlantic Avenue to Nantasket Beach.

Rowe's Wharf, our starting-point, is situated on what was called in the olden time Fort Point, in consequence of the old fortification, which stood upon Fort Hill, just inland of it, and called the Old Sconce, or South Battery. This fort was the first erected in Boston, after its settlement, by order of Governor Winthrop. Both the fort and the hill have now disappeared. Starting from the wharf, the reader will soon find himself in the stream of the main ship-channel. The first thing that will attract his attention, looking toward the northwest, is Charlestown, on which may be perceived a tall granite shaft that marks the site of the Battle of Bunker Hill.

Toward the water's edge, situated on the easterly end of Charlestown, will be perceived several large sheds, factories, and so forth, and men-of-war lying in the stream. This is the Charlestown Navy Yard. The point of land on which it is situated divides the Charles and Mystic Rivers, which here form a junction, and enter the harbor. Now, by looking to the northeast, another point of land will be observed, closely built over and surrounded by wharves and shipping, prominent among which will be observed the Cunard steamers, which can be recognized by their red funnels. This large island is known as East Boston, formerly called Noddle's Island, and probably took its name from William Noddle, whom Governor Winthrop calls "an honest man of Salem," for he was here early enough to have given to the island the name which it bore in 1630, though Mr. Samuel Maverick appears to have been a resident on it some years previous to that time.

As far back as 1631, an order was passed by the Court of Assistants, restraining persons from putting cattle, felling wood, or taking slate from Noddle's Island; and again in 1632 it was ordered "That noe pson wtsoever shall shoote att fowle vpon Noddles Ileland but that the sd place shalbe for John Perkins to take fowle with netts." But on the first of April, 1633, the following sensible order was passed by the Court: "Noddle's Ileland is granted to Mr. Samll Mauack (Maverick) to enjoy to him & heires for ever Yielding & payeing yearly att the Genrall Court to the Gounr, for the time being either a fatt weather a fatt hog or xls in money & shall giue leave to Boston & Charles Town to fetch wood contynually as their needs requires from the southerne pte of sd ileland."

Either the island was extremely well wooded at the time the order was passed, or the towns of Boston and Charlestown were very sparsely inhabited. Nowadays very little wood except chips from the ship-

BATTLE OF BUNKER HILL.

yards can be obtained from Noddle's Island, for the oldest inhabitant can only remember two trees growing upon the island previous to its purchase by the East Boston Co. in 1833. At that time the island did not contain one-tenth as many inhabitants as at the present time.

Noddle's Island was "layed to Boston" on the 9th of March, 1636-7. It originally contained six hundred and sixty-three acres. Its nearest approach to Boston is over the ship-channel by ferry, and is connected with the main land by two bridges, and with Hog Island by another. The houses on this Island were destroyed during the siege of Boston, and were rebuilt shortly after from the old barracks used by Washington's army at Cambridge.

On looking to the Southward, a long neck of land will be observed, on which are numerous churches, manufactories, and public buildings; this is South Boston, and is the neck of land described in Roger Clap's narrative as "ye neck of land called by the Indians Mattapannock," on which the settlers turned their cattle to prevent their straying, for it is connected to the main land by a narrow strip of marsh which was easily fenced. South Boston was formerly a part of Dorchester; and the high land which can be distinguished by a large square white building on it, the "Blind Asylum," is what is known in history as Dorchester Heights. On the night of March 4, 1776, Washington took possession of these Heights, where earth-works were immediately thrown up, and in the morning the British found their enemy entrenched in a strong position both for offence and defence. A fortunate storm prevented the execution of Gen. Howe's plan of dislodging the Americans, and by the 17th of March his position in Boston became so critical that an instant evacuation of the town became imperatively necessary, for these Heights commanded the town. Before noon of that day, the whole British fleet was under sail, and Gen. Washington was marching triumphantly into Boston. The British fleet anchored down the harbor, where their movements will be noticed in other chapters.

CHAPTER II.

BIRD-ISLAND SHOAL ONCE AN ISLAND AND PLACE OF EXECUTION FOR PIRATES. — WINTHROP'S OR GOVERNOR'S ISLAND IS GRANTED TO GOV. WINTHROP. — PECULIAR TERMS OF TENURE TO SAME. — PORTION OF THE ISLAND BOUGHT BY THE GOVERNMENT. — FORT WINTHROP BUILT. — DESCRIPTION OF THE FORT.

The reader is now in a fair condition to proceed down the harbor. When we say down the harbor, we do not mean beyond the Boston outer light. If we go beyond the light, we call it "going outside," which includes several shoals and sounds, and extends to the outermost rocks and ledges off the coast. Following the main ship-channel, and pursuing a southeasterly course from the starting-point, we leave Bird-Island Shoal to the left, which can be distinguished by a beacon on the easterly end. The shoal is composed of gravel and loose stones, and was formerly the site of an island, which was of some value, and contained a respectable marsh, which was mowed annually, which is confirmed by the following record taken from the old town books March 26, 1650: "Thos. Munt hath liberty to mow the marsh at Bird Island this yeare." It is also said that it was sometimes used as a place of execution and burial of pirates in the olden time. The shoal, which makes quite a show at low water, is all that now remains of the island. At high water it is all covered.

The next island to the southeast is Governor's, or, as it is sometimes called, Winthrop's Island, because the island was granted to Governor Winthrop very early by the Colonial Legislature. This noted island first took its name from Roger Conant, a distinguished early settler of Plymouth. The first known of this island is that on July 2, 1631, it was "appropriated to publique benefits and vses." But in the same month we are told the "Friendship" set sail for Christopher's Island, and ran aground behind Conant's Island, which was hard treatment for "Friendship." On the 3d of April, 1632, at a Court of Assistants, "the island called Conant's island, with all the liberties & privileges of fishing and fowleing, was demised to John Winthrop Esq. the psent Gounr., and it was further agreed that the said John Winthrop did covenant and prmise to plant a vineyard and an orchyard in the same, and that the heirs or assigns of the said John Winthrop for one & twenty yeares payeing yearely to the Gounr. the fifth parts of all such fruits & proffiits as shalbe yearly raysed out of the same, and the lease to be renewed from time to time vnto the heirs & assigns of the said John Winthrop, & the name of the said ileland was changed & is to be called the Goun'rs Garden."

It seems that the excellent Governor did not suffer the garden to go unimproved, though perhaps some of his modern successors would do so rather than keep a vineyard and provide fruit for the Legislature. It is surmised that the good old Puritan ancestors were not Prohibitionists, but had an eye to the wine vats when they looked out for the "fifth part" of the proceeds of the garden, as will be shown by the following record:—

"Whereas the yearly rent of the Goun'rs Garden was the fifth pte of all the ffruict that shall growe there, it is ordered by their present Court, (att the request of John Winthrop Esq.), that the rent of the said ileland shalbe a hogshead of the best wine that growe there to be paid yearly after the death of the said John Winthrop, and noething before."

It is to be feared that the vineyard failed, though the orchard flourished; for it appears that in 1640 a vote was passed by which John Winthrop and his heirs should pay only 2 bushels of apples each year, one bushel to the Governor & another to the generall court in winter — the same to be the best apples there growing." The records show that in the fall of the same year that Mr. Winthrop senior paid in his bushel of apples to the General Court, and the other bushel to Thomas Dudley, his successor in office that year. It is supposed that the apples were faithfully paid in every year, and that each of the members of the General Court carried home his pockets full; for again in 1642 the following significant entry appears on the records: "The bushell of apples was

FORT WINTHROP.

paid in." How long this practice continued is not known; certainly it did not reach to modern times, for it would have been hard for some years past to find any apples except "apples, of the earth," with which to have fulfilled the contract.

The island continued in the possession of the Winthrop family till 1808, when a portion of it was sold to the Government for the purpose of erecting a fort, which, when built, was called Fort Warren, in respect to Gen. Joseph Warren. This name, however, has since been transferred to another fort erected on George's Island; and the new fortification now in process of erection on the summit of the high hill on the island has been named Fort Winthrop, in remembrance of the first Governor to whom it was first granted. The fort which is now in process of construction is of great strength. It has a commanding position, and the batteries are nearly all underground, and connected with the Citadel (the top of which can be seen on the highest part of the island) with underground passages, and the water battery that will be observed on the southerly side of the island is of great advantage to the defence, controlling as it does a large extent of flats which are very shoal except at the highest tides. Although the defences of this island do not show very much from the water front on account of their being underground, yet on this very account it will be almost impregnable when finished, and will be by far the strongest fortress in the harbor.

CHAPTER III.

ATTEMPT TO LOCATE A FORT IN THE HARBOR. — FORT AT CASTLE ISLAND UNDERTAKEN. — DESCRIPTION OF THE FORT BY CAPT. JOHNSTON AND CAPT. ROGER CLAP. — THE CASTLE ABANDONED. — ARRIVAL OF LA TOUR AND FRIGHT OF THE INHABITANTS. — CASTLE BURNT. — DESTROYED BY THE BRITISH. — REBUILT AND CALLED FORT INDEPENDENCE. — EXECUTIONS THERE DURING THE REBELLION.

Having passed Fort Winthrop by way of the main ship-channel, the next island we will notice will be Castle Island, which is directly opposite to Fort Winthrop to the southward, and can be easily recognized by the granite fortress and earthwork, it being one of the most prominent forts in Boston Harbor. Very soon after the settlement of Boston the civil authorities began to consider the question of erecting defences in the harbor, in addition to the fort on Fort Hill. The first place thought of was Hull, at the entrance to the harbor; and an expedition to the same is thus chronicled by Governor Winthrop in his valuable journal, February, 1632:—

"The Governr & 4 of the Assistants, with 3 of the Ministrs & others, about 26 in all, went in 3 boats to view Nantaskott the wind W., faire weather; but the winde arose N. W. so strong & extreme colde, that they were kept there 2 nights, being forced to lodge vpon the ground, in an open cottage, vpon a little olde strawe, which they pulled from the thache. Their victualls allso grewe shorte, so they were forced to eat muskles, yet they were very weary, & came all safe home, the 3 days after, throughe the Lord's spec'lle providence. Vpon view of the place it was agreed by all that to build a fort there it would be too great charge & of little vse wherevpon the planting of that place was deferred."

Not satisfied with the failure above recited, the same party that went to Nantasket made another attempt a year later, for Mr. Winthrop relates as follows: —

"The Governr & Council, & divers of the Minrs, & others, met at Castle Island, & there agreed vpon erecting 2 platformes & one small forti-

THE CASTLE, OR FORT INDEPENDENCE.

fication to secure them bothe, & for the present furtherance of it they agreed to lay out 5 *li* a man till a rate might be made at the Genll Court. The Deputye Roger Ludlowe was chosen overseer of the worke."

To show its earnestness in this endeavor, the General Court passed a vote, "That the ffort att Castle Island, nowe begun shalbe fully pfcted, the ordinance mounted & eury other thing aboute it ffinished before any other ffortificacon be further proceeded in."

Captain Edward Johnson of Woburn, in his "Wonder-Working Providence of Sion's Saviour," printed in 1654, speaks of the fort on Castle Island as follows: —

"The Castle is built on the northeast of the Island, upon a rising hill, very advantageous to make many shot at such ships as shall offer to enter the harbor without their good leave and liking; the Commander of it is one Captain Davenport, a man approved for his faithfulness, and skill; the master cannoneer is an active engineer; also the castle hath cost about four thousand pounds, yet are not this poor pilgrim people weary of maintaining it in good repair, it is of very good use to awe any insolent persons, that putting confidence in their ships and sails, shall offer any injury to the people or contemn their government, and they have certain signals of alarums which suddenly spread through the whole country."

Captain Roger Clap, who commanded the fort twenty-one years, gives the following description of the fort: —

"I will inform you that God stirred up his poor servants to use means in the begining for their preservation; though a low and weak people, yet a willing people to lay out their estates for the defence of themselves and others, they having friends in divers places who thought it best for our safety to build a fort upon the island now called Castle Island; at first they built a castle with mud walls which stood divers years: First Capt Simkins was commander thereof, and after him, Lieut Morris, for a little space. When the mud walls failed, it was built again with pine trees and earth; and Capt Davenport was commander, when that decayed which was in a little time there was a small castle built with brick walls, and had three rooms in it; dwelling room below, lodging room over it, and the gun room over that, wherein stood six very good Saker Guns, and over it on the top three lesser guns. All the time of our weakness God was pleased to give us peace, until the wars with the Dutch in Charles II's time. At that time our works were very weak, and intelligence came to us that Durother, a Dutch commander of a squadron of ships, was in the West Indies, and did intend to visit us, whereupon our Battery also was repaired, wherein are seven good guns, but in the very time of this report in July 1665, God was pleased to send a grevious storm of thunder & lightening, which did some hurt at Boston and struck dead here at Castle Island that worthy renowned Captain Richard Davenport; upon which the General Court in Aug. 10th following appointed another (Roger Clap himself) Captain in room of him that was slain. But behold God wrought for us; Durother intended to come here yet God by contrary winds kept him out, so he went to Newfoundland and did great spoil there."

During the administration of Lieu. Morris an affair took place which will clearly illustrate the manner of doing things in the olden time.

"Three ships arrived here from Ipswich with three hundred and sixty passengers, the last being loath to come to anchor at Castle Island though hailed by the castle boat and required etc. The gunner made a shot before her for a warning, but the powder in the touchole being wet and the ship having fresh way with wind and tide, the shot took place in the shrouds and killed a passenger an honest man. The next day the governor charged an inquest, and sent them aboard with two of the magistrates to take view of the dead body, and who having all the evidence, found that he came to his death by the providence of God."

This verdict of the jury of inquest undoubtedly gave great satisfaction to Lieu. Morris and his gunner, and to the staid townsmen of Boston, but proved of little account to the poor man who had lost his life, or to the fellow-passengers who had to be thankful that they had escaped a similar providence.

The Castle at last went to decay, and was abandoned, but the inhabitants of Boston, as well as their Governors, were very much alarmed, for on the 4th of June, 1634, there arrived in the harbor a ship of 140 tons, having on board the same number of persons. The Governor and his family were on their island when M. La Tour came up the harbor in his ship. The neighboring towns of Boston and Charlestown betook them to their arms, and three shallops with armed men went forth to meet the Governor, and to guard him to his house in town. The Goverernor in his journal says : —

"But here the Lord gave us occasion to notice our weakness, for if La Tour had been illminded towards us, he had such an opportunity as we hope neither he nor any other shall ever have the like again; for coming to our castle and saluting it, there was none to answer him, for the last Court had given orders to have Castle Island deserted, a great part of the work being fallen down, &c. So he might have taken all the ordnance there, then having the Governor and his family, and Capt. Gibbon's wife etc in his power, he might have gone and spoiled Boston, and having so many men ready they might have taken two ships in the harbor and gone away without danger or resistance."

This fright produced a good effect, for measures were immediately taken for renewing the fortification on Castle Island. The towns in the vicinity of Boston were each assessed their portion toward defraying the expense of constructing the fort, and it was decided that the garrison should "consist of twenty men for the summer season, and ten for the winter. The captain to receive forty pounds for his house, and one hundred for the fort; and he was told as no constant minister could be expected, and as the Lord having furnished him with able gifts, he is to take care of the garrison as his own family and that only one half in turn can come up to town on the Lord's day and he himself every other Sunday, that he should have one third of the island for his own use, one tenth for his gunner, and the remainder for the garrison; that he shall send a boat to examine every ship that approacheth the town, that he could cut wood from any of the islands not disposed of, and that all trading vessels should come and depart unmolested."

About this time the armament and military property of the fort consisted of six murthers, two boats, a drum, two muskets, and a suitable number of pikes for each soldier. On March 21, 1672, the Castle, being chiefly built of wood, took fire, and was entirely destroyed. A new fort was built in 1674, which remained without much of any change till 1701, when the old works were demolished, and new ones, built of brick in a very substantial manner, were erected in their place, and over its entrance was placed the following inscription: —

"In the thirteenth year of the reign of William the Third, most invincible King of Great Britain, France and Ireland, this fortification was undertaken; and was finished in the second year of the reign of the most serene Ann, Queen of Great Britain, France and Ireland, and in the year of our Lord 1703. Built by Col. William Wolfgang Romer, chief military engineer to their royal majesties in North America."

A portion of this instructive stone is in a good state of preservation, and a small portion of the old wall has been retained in constructing the rear portion of the present fort, Fort Indepencence; but, as it is covered with granite ashlers, it is hidden from sight.

When the British evacuated Boston, they destroyed Castle William; and, after the provincial forces took possession, they repaired it, and its name was changed to Fort Independence in 1797, President John Adams being present on the occasion. The Castle was noted for years as a duelling ground. A memorial of one of these unfortunate affairs can now be seen standing on the glacis of the fort, on which is the following inscription: —

Near this spot
on the 25th Dec. 1817
fell
LIEU. ROBERT F. MASSIE
Aged 21 years.

The Castle was used as a place of confinement for thieves and other convicts sentenced to hard labor, from 1785 till the State's Prison in Charlestown was built in 1805. Within a few years a substantial stone fort has been erected in place of old Castle William. During our late civil war a number of prisoners were confined here, and several deserters were executed by being shot.

CHAPTER IV.

APPLE ISLAND. — USED AS A MARINE RESIDENCE. — IS OWNED BY THOMAS HUTCHINSON, ESTES HATCH, JAMES MORTIMER, WILLIAM MARSH. — HOUSE BURNT IN 1835. — THE ISLAND PURCHASED BY THE CITY. — FAVORITE RESORT FOR CAMPING PARTIES.

Having passed Governor's Island and the Castle, Apple Island will be observed to the northeast of Governor's Island, about a mile distant. The island is round, gently rising from its shores to its centre, and has a considerable show of trees upon it, two of which have been the most prominent objects in the harbor for many years, attracting the eye in the daytime much more readily than the lighthouse on Long-Island Head. The flats that surround it are very extensive, and make its approach at low tide very difficult. This small green spot in the harbor soon fell under the jurisdiction of Boston, and in the early days of the town it was used, as most of the other islands were, for pasturage of sheep and cattle; but in later times, having a richer soil, and being less exposed to the storms, than the other islands, it became desirable for a marine residence, and as such was improved previous to the war of the Revolution. From being the property of the town, Apple Island passed into private hands, and in 1723 was sold by Hon. Thomas Hutchinson to Mr. Estes Hatch, together with the housings, edifices, and buildings thereon, for the sum of £200. The executor of Mr. Hatch sold it in 1750 to Mr. James Mortimer, of Boston, tallow-chandler, for the sum of £133. 6s. 8d. To give some idea of the island at the time of Mr.

Mortimer's decease in 1773, the following extract is taken from his will: —

Apple Island, so called, in Boston Harbor, and with the building thereon	£200
About ten tons of hay	15
An old mare £6, mare colt 2 years old £10	16
A horse colt 10 weeks old	3
A dray cart 10s, a hand cart 10s	1
A large boat and apparatus with cordage £6, a small do. 12s.	6. 12s.

£241. 12s.

The island remained in the possession of the Mortimer family and their descendents for many years, till it finally descended to Mr. Robert Wilcox, living at North Shields, in Northumberlandshire, England, who knew but little about it, and probably placed but little value on it, and consequently suffered the house to decay, and the trees to waste. In this state of things this romantic spot was selected by an English gentleman by the name of William Marsh as a place of residence, and in the year 1814, at the close of the war, he placed his family there. After making the fields smile, and the gardens rejoice, the first object of Mr. Marsh was to find the legal owner of the island, that he might become the lawful possessor of what he deemed a modern Eden. In his search he was not successful till he had striven many years. About the year 1822, however, he obtained possession of the knowledge of the person who appeared to be the owner, and he made with him an agreement by which he was to pay five hundred dollars for the island, and become the rightful owner of his much-desired residence. So careful and yet so scrupulously honest was he in this transaction, that he required the legal proofs of the identity of Robert Wilcox, the reputed owner. This evidence he did not obtain till 1830, a few years before his decease, when the purchase money was paid, and the deeds passed and recorded.

Mr. Marsh seems to have passed a happy and contented life on the island, secure from intrusion on account of its difficulty of approach, and enjoying the position on account of the fertility of the soil and its neighborhood to good fishing grounds and fields for sporting life. He died in 1833, at the good old age of sixty-six, and was buried, at his own request, on the western slope of the hill upon his own beloved island, a large number of friends being present on the mournful occasion. Many persons will undoubtedly remember his faithful negro servant, Black Jack, who was so infamously treated by some of the navy officers stationed in the harbor, for assisting a man, as they alleged, to desert; and the successful endeavors of Samuel McCleary, who took charge of the case, and recovered for him damages for the abuse.

Since the decease of Mr. Marsh, and the burning of the house, which occurred in 1835, the island has passed into other hands; and, after many years' neglect, the city purchased the island in 1867, paying 3,750 dollars for it. It is not now put to any useful or remunerative purpose; but it is held solely for the prevention of the removal of the gravel and ballast stones which are found upon it. Occasionally an old hulk is broken up, and burned on the flats for the saving of the iron and copper used in its construction.

There is no spot in the harbor which offers so strong an invitation for a delightful place as a marine rural residence during the sultry summer season. It is also an excellent place for camping parties and clambakes. Clams are found there in great abundance on the flats that surround the island.

CHAPTER V.

PRESIDENT'S ROAD. — LOWER MIDDLE. — THOMPSON'S ISLAND. — STANDISH VISITS THE ISLAND IN 1621. — IS SETTLED BY DAVID THOMPSON IN 1626. — THE ISLAND IS GRANTED TO DORCHESTER. — CLAIMED BY JOHN THOMPSON IN 1648. — TESTIMONY OF THE SAGAMORE OF AGAWAM AND OTHERS. — THE ISLAND SOLD TO THE FARM-SCHOOL CORPORATION, AND ANNEXED TO BOSTON IN 1834.

Having now reached the entrance to the President's road, which was in olden time called King's road, exactly north of which is the Lower Middle, a gravelly, rocky shoal, which is sometimes, at very low water, exposed to view, directly toward the south will be observed Thompson's Island, which can be recognized by the Farm-School building, barn, wharf, orchard, and so forth.

This is one of the best-cultivated and most fruitful islands in the harbor, and one thing that distinguishes it from all others is the growth of trees which is now beginning to make quite a show on the island, and which all the other islands are so sadly deficient in. Thompson's Island is about one mile in length from northeast to southwest, and about a third of a mile in width, and contains about a hundred and forty acres of land suitable for agricultural purposes. It is about half a mile north of Squantum, a well-known promontory of North Quincy, the nearest point of the main land to the island. The surface is gently rising, forming two eminences, which are called East and West heads; and between these on the southeasterly side is a cove, and on the southwesterly side a salt-water pond of several acres, from which once flowed a creek that in ancient times was dignified by the name of river. The creek has this year (1879) had a dike built across it, and the pond drained so as to make meadow-land of it, when it will yield bountiful crops from its rich alluvial soil.

The bar which projects from the southern extreme of the island, about a quarter of a mile toward Squantum, has long been a noted locality, furnishing delicious clams, in greater profusion than any other place the writer has seen on the entire coast. The clams were considered of so much account by the inhabitants of Dorchester, that, when the island was set off by an act of the Legislature in 1834 from the town of Dorchester to the city of Boston, it was enacted " that it should not destroy or affect any lawful right that the inhabitants of Dorchester might have of digging and taking clams on the banks of the said island," evidently showing that its flats had not lost their value in respect to the famous New-England shell-fish.

This island was one of the first settled places in Boston Harbor. It was occupied by Mr. David Thompson some years previous to the settlement of Boston. He had been sent out in 1623, by Sir Fernando Gorges, to trade with the Indians at Piscataqua; but, being discontented, he removed to Boston Harbor, and selected this island on account of its proximity to the Massachusetts Indians, whose principal village was situated on the Neponset River, but a short distance from the island. This tribe was noted hunters, and the ponds and streams in the Blue Hills, flowing into the Neponset River, abounded with beaver, otter, mink, and other fur-bearing animals. Mr. Thompson erected a trading-post on the island, where he did a lucrative business with the Indians. He is supposed to have died on the island in 1628, leaving an only son, John, an infant, who inherited his estate, which also included Squantum. This island has always been private property since the time of the Thompsons, and used for purposes connected with agriculture; although after the settlement of Dorchester and Boston, it was granted by the General Court of the Colony to the town of Dorchester, in the following words, under date of 1634: "Thompson's Island is granted to the inhabitants of Dorchestr to enjoy to them and their heires & successors wch shall inhabite there foreuer payeing the yearely rent of xij*d* to the treasurer for the time being."

The town of Dorchester voted that a rent of twenty pounds a year should be charged for the Island, to be paid by the tenants toward the maintenance of a school in Dorchester; this rent "to bee payd to such schoolemaster as shall vundertake to teach English, Latine, and other tongues, and also writing." So it seems that the good people of Dorchester early provided for schools where the really solid branches should be taught. The difficulty of collecting rent, however, induced the town to provide that there should be but ten tenants upon the island at one time.

These halcyon days, however, did not last forever; for Mr. John Thompson, the son of David Thompson, made claim to it, and the town lost it, as will appear from the Colony records of May 10, 1648. "Forasmuch as it appears to this Corte, upon the petition of Mr. John Thompson, sonn & heir of David Thompson, deceased, that the said David, in or about the year 1626, did take actuall possession of an iland in the Massachusetts Bay, called Thomson's Iland, & then being vacuum domicilium, & before the patent granted to us of the Massachusetts Bay & did erect there the form of an habitation, & dying soone after, leaving the petitioner an infant, who so soone as he came of age, did make his claim formally, & now againe by his said petition, this Corte, considring the premises, & not willing to deprive any of their lawful rights and possessions, or to prmit any piudice to come to the petionr in the time of his nonage, do hereby grant the said iland, called Thompson's

THOMPSON'S ISLAND.

Iland, to the said John Thompson & his heirs forever, to belong to this jurisdiction, & to be undr the govrnment & laws thereof."

This was the first law-case of importance that occurred in the colony; and the town, not satisfied with the result of the petition, tried again to get the island restored by law, but failed in the attempt. When Mr. John Thompson made his defence against the renewed claim of the town to the island, in 1650, he brought in evidence certain affidavits of William Trevore, William Blackstone, Myles Standish, and the Sagamore of Agawam, all eminent persons in their way. These documents, copies of which are preserved, make it appear, that, early after the settlement of Plymouth, Captain Standish and others, among whom was William Trevore, a sailor, who came over in the "Mayflower" in 1620, visited Boston Harbor in September, 1621, and was one of the party that explored the harbor and interviewed the Indians, and at that time Trevore took possession of the island under the name of Island of Trevore, for Mr. David Thompson, then of London, and that Mr. Thompson obtained a grant of the island before the arrival of the Massachusetts Company.

Mr. Blackstone, who was known as the first European resident in Boston, and whom Blackstone Street was named after, stated that he knew "ould Mr. Thompson;" that he affirmed that he "had a patten for it," and that there is a "harbour in the island for a boat, which none of the rest of the islands had." The Sagamore of Agawam testified as follows: "I Saggamore of Agamam testify that in the year 1619 or thereabouts, as I remember, I went in my own person, with Mr. David Thompson and he took possession of the Iland before Dorchester, he liking no other but that because of the smale Riuer, and then no Indians upon it or any wigwam or planting, nor hath been by any Endians inhabitted or claymed since, but two years ago by Harmben an old Endian of Dorchester."

In 1834, the island was purchased by the Farm-School corporation, an institution incorporated in 1733 by the merchants of Boston for the purpose of founding a home for indigent boys of American parentage to teach them farming, and give them a good common-school education. In the same year it was set off, by an act of the Legislature, from the town of Dorchester, with which it had been connected for two hundred years, and annexed to Boston. This school is often mistaken for a reformatory institution, something after the style of the State Reform School at Westboro; but it is an entirely different institution, for the boys must be of good character in order to be admitted here, and the school is supported by private enterprise, is now nearly self-supporting, and is not a public institution.

THOMPSON'S TRADING HOUSE.

CHAPTER VI.

POSITION AND FORM OF SPECTACLE ISLAND. — SIZE OF THE ISLAND. — FORMERLY COVERED WITH WOOD. — LAID OUT FOR PLANTERS. — PURCHASED BY THOMAS BILL. — INDIAN CLAIM AND RELEASE IN 1684. — IS USED FOR QUARANTINE. — FREQUENTED BY EXCURSIONISTS. — PRESENT USE OF THE ISLAND.

Continuing our course down the President's road and looking in a southerly direction, the reader will come to a peculiarly shaped island called Spectacle Island, from its remarkable resemblance to a pair of spectacles; it being formed of two peninsulas connected together by a short bar which is covered with water at high tide. It lies between Thompson's and Long Island, and is south of the President's road. It is estimated to contain about sixty acres of land. The first mention of this noted locality in the records is in 1634, when, "together with Deer Island, Hog Island, and Long Island, it was granted to the town of Boston, for the yearly rent of four shillings, for the four islands," which may be called one shilling apiece for each of them. Very soon after it came into the possession of the town, it was allotted to the different inhabitants, who paid a small annual rent, to inure to the benefit of the free school. At this time the island was well covered with wood; for in January, 1687, about thirty persons of Boston went out on a fair day to Spectacle Island to cut wood, the town being in great want thereof. The next night the wind rose very high at the northeast, with snow, and afterward at the northwest, for two days, and it was so cold that the harbor froze over, except a small channel. These thirty adventurers met with hard luck; for, of their number, twelve could get no farther home than Governor's Island. Seven were carried in the ice in a small skiff through Broad Sound, to the Brewsters, where they had to stay two days without food and fire, and get home by way of Pulling Point (Point Shirley); and many of the others, after detention, had their limbs frozen, and one died.

In 1649, the town began to take measures for granting the land at the island to planters for perpetuity, reserving the exaction of a small annual rent of about sixpence an acre for the benefit of the free schools; and in April of that year, ten persons bound "themselves and their successors to pay sixpence an acre p yeare for their land at Spectacle iland, foreuer to ye use of the schole, yt soe it maye be proprietye to them for euer, and they are to bring in their pay to the townes treasurer the first day of February for eu or else their land is forfeit into the townes dispossing." These persons did not pay their rent as promptly as they should, and some of them conveyed their rights to others, insomuch that there were large arrearages due, and the treasurers were authorized to levey and collect by help of the constable. About ten years later, the town relinquished all its rights to the planters, and made void its agreement about its annual rent of a sixpence an acre for the benefit of the school, on condition that the back rent should be paid up in full to that date. This was undoubtedly done; for, just previous to this, Mr. Thomas Bill, a lighterman, began to buy up the rights of the several owners, and when he had nearly acquired the whole island he sold his thirty-five acres to his son Samuel Bill, a butcher, who had previously purchased five acres of Mr. John Slater (part of his inheritance from his father, William, a mariner), and also other parts of several persons. Thus he thought he became owner of the whole island; but here an Indian claim turned up, and had to be quieted. It appears that the new claimant was Charles Josiah, the son of Wampatuck, late sachem of the Massachusetts, and grandson of Chickataubut.

This distinguished individual says, in the deed of release, "for divers good causes and considerations me thereunto moving, & in particular for and in consideration of money to me in hand paid, before the unsealing of this deed, by Samuel Bill, of Boston, butcher, have with ye knowledge and consent of my wise men and councillors, Wm. Ahaton Senr, Wm. Ahaton Junr, & Robert Momentaug, given, granted, sold, enfeoffed and confirmed, one certain island scituate in the Massachusetts Bay commonly known and called by the name of Spectacle Island, in the present possession of the same Bill." The Indian covenants in the deed "that (according to Indian right & title) he is the sole owner and proprietor of the sd island." At the decease of Samuel Bill, his property on the island consisted of house, seventy-six sheep, two cows, two negro men, a boat, one old mare, one hog, tools, and so forth. The whole amounting to £144, 18s. 8d. The island remained in the possession of the Bill family till a portion of it, the southerly end, was sold to the Province in 1717 for the sum of £100, in bills of credit, for the purpose of erecting a "Pest House there for the reception & entertainment of sick persons, coming from beyond the Sea, and in order to prevent the spreading of Infection."

Things must have gone on slowly at the island; for in 1720 it was voted "that the selectmen of the town of Boston be desired to take care for the furnishing of the Public Hospital on Spectacle Island, so as to make it warm and comfortable for the entertainment of the sick."

From this time things went along well till 1736, when the hospital was removed to Rainsford's Island, and Spectacle Island again reverted back to the Bill family, who retained possession of the island till 1741, when it was sold to Edward Bromfield, Esq.; and since then Spectacle Island has not been improved for public use, but has been used for the purpose of agriculture and pasturage, and for a number of years the father of Mr. William Reed, now the proprietor of Squantum, kept a house of entertainment on the island for persons going on pleasure excursions down the harbor, and many of the old yachtsmen will remember the genial countenance of this pioneer in the hotel business in Boston Harbor.

Of late years the island has been put to a new business, which speaks for itself if the reader happens to be to the leeward of it: "it resembles not the odors that are wafted on the summer breezes from the spice islands." A vessel named after its proprietor, the "Nahum Ward," plies between the city and the island, loaded with dead horses, which, when passed through certain processes of manipulation, yield a valuable return, although the island, in consequence, has ceased to be a place of resort as formerly.

CHAPTER VII.

LONG ISLAND. — ANCIENT DESCRIPTION, FORM, AND DIMENSIONS. — GRANTED TO BOSTON IN 1634, AND LAID OUT IN LOTS IN 1640. — CLAIM OF THE EARL OF STIRLING. — IN POSSESSION OF JOHN NELSON. — BOUGHT BY THE LONG-ISLAND COMPANY. — DESCRIPTION OF THE LIGHT-HOUSE. — REDOUBT BUILT THERE DURING THE REVOLUTION. — PORTUGUESE VILLAGE OF FISHERMEN. — USED DURING THE REBELLION FOR A CONSCRIPT CAMP. — ITS PRESENT CONDITION AND FUTURE PROSPECTS.

The next island to the eastward of Spectacle Island is Long Island, so called from its extreme length, which is greater than that of any other island in the harbor. It is about a mile and three-quarters in length from northeast to southwest, and about a quarter of a mile wide. It can be readily distinguished, on passing it, by the large hotel situated in nearly the centre of the island, and known as the Long-Island House, surrounded by well-kept grounds, on which are a number of fine trees, which are so scarce on all the islands in the harbor.

The following account, written in 1635 by Mr. William Wood in his "New-England Prospect," hardly seems to apply at the present day: —

"These Iles abound with Woods, and Water, and Meadow-ground; and whatsoever the spacious fertile Maine affords. The inhabitants use to put their Cattle, in these for safety viz their Rammes, Goates, and Swine, when their Corne is on the ground."

The history of this island bears a strong resemblance to that of many others in the harbor. It was granted to Boston, together with Deer

Island and Hog Island, in April, 1634, for the annual rent of two pounds for the three. Very soon after the acquirement of the island, the town of Boston began to apportion it out to various persons for improvement; and the felling of the trees, with which it was well wooded on the arrival of the first settlers of the town, took place in real earnest, and it was not long before it was so divested of its forests as to become only fit for the pasturage of cattle, sheep, and swine.

In February, 1639, at a town meeting, it was directed that the island should be laid out into lots for planters, the record of which is to be found in the first volume of the town records, on the fortieth page, and reads as follows: —

"At this meeting o'r brother Edward Rainsford & Willyam Hudson are appointed to accompany ye surveyor to lay out the planting ground at Long Iland & they are to beginne at the east end; & if any have bestowed any labor vpon yt wch shall fall to another man, he who shall enjoy ye benefitt thereof shall eyther allow for ye charge, or cleare so much for ye other."

Here we find an early practical application of the principle of the betterment law, with a view of fair treatment of pre-occupants and squatters. The affairs were managed on this island precisely the same as on Spectacle Island; the town relinquishing the island to the planters, they to pay a yearly rent to be applied to the benefit of the free schools. The planters not paying, the constable was sent to them to distrain for the rent. Failing in this, the island was sold, and passed into private hands, free of all encumbrances.

Most of the islands in the harbor had at some period of their history claimants in the shape of Indians; but Long Island was claimed by no less a dignitary than the Right Honorable William, Earl of Sterling, who in 1641 recorded a protest by his agent, James Forrett, against Edward Tomlins and others as intruders on Long Island. This claim was not sustained, and the title proved good to the grantees from the town.

In course of time, the title became vested, by purchase of the renters, in Mr. John Nelson of Boston, the heroic person who in 1689, at the head of the soldiery, made Sir Edmund Andros surrender himself and the fort on Fort Hill to the incensed colonists whose rights he was then usurping. Mr. Nelson was a patriot of considerable note in his day. He was a near relative to Sir Thomas Temple, who figured quite prominently this side of the Atlantic in colony times.

FISHERMEN'S HOUSES, LONG ISLAND.

The island passed through various hands till 1847. Then the Long-Island Company bought all the island except the East Head, built a substantial wharf, and erected the Long-Island House, laid out streets, and cut the land up into building-lots, and started a real-estate speculation on the island, which, however, did not succeed, for but a few buildings were erected.

In 1819 a lighthouse was erected on the East Head. Its tower is twenty-two feet in height, and is built of iron, painted white, with a black lantern containing nine burners, and is about eighty feet above the level of the sea, and shows a white fixed light that can be seen on a clear night about fifteen miles. It has for its object the guidance of vessels up the roads of the harbor. It is situated in a square enclosure of ground on the summit of the Head. Within the square is a comfortable stone house for the keeper, and a remarkably good well of water.

LONG-ISLAND LIGHT.

Near the lighthouse was the redoubt erected by Washington's army during the Revolutionary War for the purpose of driving the British fleet out of the harbor, where they remained after the evacuation of Boston. The redoubt was destroyed a few years ago to make place for the more extensive fortification now in process of construction on the summit of the Head.

The prospect from this Head is surpassed by none that can be obtained from any of the eminences upon the other islands in the harbor. The head was fast disappearing from the effects of storms and currents till recently, when the U. S. Government erected a substantial sea-wall around it, thus protecting it from the encroachments of the sea.

On the southeasterly side of the island is a cove which is used as a harbor by the fishermen for their small boats. It is protected from the rough water by a projecting beach, which is fast being washed away. Near this small harbor is quite a fishing village inhabited mostly by Portuguese, who have superseded the native American fishermen on account of their cheap way of living, which is a very similar case to that of the Chinese on the Pacific coast.

The fishing is now done to a great extent all along the New-England coast by Portuguese; not that they are any better fishermen or as good as the native American, but on account of their working cheaper. Excursionists can go ashore here and purchase fresh boiled lobsters at an exceedingly low price.

Long Island is one of the pleasantest islands in the harbor for summer residences, and will in time probably prove a desirable resort for such purposes, unless the city takes possession of the island, and removes the various city institutions to it, which may be the case in the course of time, as the matter is now under consideration.

During the Rebellion the island was used as a conscript camp, and rendezvous for Massachusetts soldiers previous to their being mustered into the service of the United States.

During the last century the island was used for farming purposes, and families resided upon it; but lately it has been put to but little use except for pasturage.

CHAPTER VIII.

DEER ISLAND. — ITS SIZE, HILLS, BLUFFS, AND PONDS. — ORIGIN OF ITS NAME. — IT SUPPLIES FIREWOOD TO THE INHABITANTS OF BOSTON. — USED AS A PRISON FOR SWINE AND GOATS. — JOHN RUGGLES BUILDS ON THE ISLAND. — LEASED TO SIR THOMAS TEMPLE. — DESTRUCTION OF ALL THE FOREST ON THE ISLAND. — THE SACHEM WAMPATUCK AND OTHER INDIANS CLAIM THE ISLAND. — SIR EDMUND ANDROS ATTEMPTS TO TAKE POSSESSION OF THE ISLAND. — IS NOW USED FOR THE CITY INSTITUTIONS.

Deer Island lies directly north of the East Head of Long Island, between which is the main ship-channel. It is separated from the town of Winthrop by Shirley Gut, a passage the narrowest part of which measures about three hundred and twenty-five feet. The island is nearly a mile in width, and contains about one hundred and thirty-four acres of upland and fifty acres of marsh, making one hundred and eighty-four acres in all. Besides a large amount of flats more than equal to all the upland and marsh, it has two hills and four bluffs which are known by the names of North Head, East Head, and South Head (or Money Head), Graveyard Bluff (a small projection on the southwesterly part of the island), and Signal Hill in the central part of the island. The South Head took the name of Money Head in consequence of the money-digging affair that occurred there some years ago. North and south of Signal Hill are two small fresh-water ponds; the northerly known as Ice Pond, and the southerly as Cow Pond, — the former generally supplying the occupants of the island with ice for the summer months, and the latter affording refreshing water for the cattle.

Deer Island took its name from the fact that deer formerly visited and occupied its ancient groves, which have long since been cut down for fuel and lumber. Mr. William Wood, in his "New-England Prospect," printed in 1634, says, —

"The chiefe Islands which keep out the Winde and Sea from disturbing the Harbours, are first Deare Iland, which lies within a flight-shot of Pulling point. This Iland is so called, because of the Deare which often swimme thither from the Maine, when they are chased by the Woolves: Some have killed sixteene Deare in a day upon this Iland. The opposite shore is called Pulling point, because that is the usuall Channel Boats use to passe thorow into the Bay; and the Tyde being very strong, they are constrayned to goe a-shore, and hale their Boats by the seasing, or roades, whereupon, it was called Pulling point."

What was known formerly as "Pulling Point" is now called Point Shirley, on which is built the Point-Shirley House, commonly known as Taft's, and celebrated for the game dinners served there.

In 1634, this island, together with Long Island and Hog Island, were granted in perpetuity to Boston for the nominal rent of two pounds; and this amount was reduced to four shillings, and Spectacle Island thrown in beside, and the original grant was confirmed by the Colonial Legislature. Then terminated all the right of the colony to the island, and the Province and Commonwealth has never set up any claim since to its territory, but the ownership has remained vested in the town and city of Boston.

At this time the island appears to have been of no special use to the inhabitants except to procure fire-wood from; for an order was passed in 1636, as follows: —

"Also it is agreed yt ye Inhabitants who doe want wood, shall have liberty to gett for their vse at Deare Island, so as yt they psently take & carrye away what they doe gett, & whatsoeuer they have felled there to be at liberty for others to take away."

If they had known the mischief that would ensue from this order, it is very questionable whether they would have passed it; for now it is with the greatest difficulty that trees can be made to grow upon the island, on account of the easterly sea-winds which are so unpropitious

POINT SHIRLEY.

to their cultivation. A few willows and silver-leaf poplars of quite recent planting are now the only trees on the island.

In 1641, an order was passed by the town, authorizing that trespassing swine which should be suffered to roam about the town insufficiently yoked, and goats found without a keeper, should be sentenced to Deer Island for a time. Now a different kind of trespassers are sent there, that have proved to be of more trouble to the city than the swine and goats, inasmuch as they have transgressed the laws knowingly. John

Ruggles then put up a building on the island to be used as a pound for swine and goats, for which he received the sum of £7, 15s. 6d.

An order was passed in 1644, to lease the island to James Penn and John Oliver for three years, at the rate of seven pounds a year. The income of the island was applied to school purposes. The inhabitants of the town were still granted the privilege of cutting wood on the island, provided that they carried it off, or set it on heaps, "that it might not be spoyled, nor hinder the feed of cattell."

Mr. Edward Bendall next leased it for a term of twenty-one years, he to leave at the end of his term a supply of wood for the maintenance of one family forever, and also fruit trees he should plant there; but, as Mr. Bendall did not pay his rent there, the constable was sent to distrain for the rent, and a month later Mr. James Bill was debarred from cutting any more wood there, as there only remained enough for a farm.

The constable seems to have had lively times among the inhabitants of the different islands; for none of them seem to have been able to pay their rent.

In 1662, Sir Thomas Temple leased the island for thirty-one years, at the rate of fourteen pounds a year, to be applied to school purposes; and he is allowed "to clear the swamp on the said island of all timber trees whatever, and allsoe what other woode is vpon the said island, excepting some timber trees," and so, probably, came to an end all the trees which formerly grew upon the island.

About this time several of the Massachusetts Indians laid claim to Deer Island. This claim was met with in a conciliatory manner by the townsmen of Boston, who appointed a person to arrange with the Indians, and purchase their claim. Wampatuck and three other Indians executed a quit-claim to the selectmen of the town of the property claimed, acknowledging that his grandfather, Chickataubut, had about fifty-five years previous sold the the island to English planters and settlers. At the same time, David, son and heir of Sagamore George, relinquished the right which he claimed to Deer Island. At this time Mr. Samuel Shrimpton, an extensive land owner, had become possessed of Sir Thomas Temple's lease. The town renewed the lease for 18 years on the same terms, he having paid £19 to the sachem and other Indians for ratifying the ancient grant of Chickataubut.

Not long after this, the intolerant and troublesome Sir Edmund Andros, who unrightfully held the position of Governor of New England, caused writs to be issued against the tenant, which the town determined to resist; and, finally, the usurper was seized and imprisoned. But fortunately, the revolution occurring in England, the whole matter ceased, and the town and its tenant were left in quiet possession of the island, which the town has continued to hold, without further hindrance, until the present time.

The island is now used by the city as a place for its institutions, such as the House of Industry, which was removed from South Boston in 1848, and the House of Reformation and Alms-House, which were removed from the same place in 1858. The large brick building which forms one of the principal land-marks in the harbor was built in 1850. In 1869, a building for a farm-house, and another for pauper girls, were erected.

A considerable portion of the easterly shore of this island having been washed away in storms, a sea-wall has been erected there for its better protection, and that of the harbor, which is much injured by the washings from the bluffs of this and other islands. So great is the wear from the headlands of Deer Island, that quite an extensive bar has been created by the above-named cause, extending a considerable distance from its northerly point toward Gut Plain upon Point Shirley, and another called Fawn Bar, from its easterly head toward the ledge of rock known as the Graves, in an easterly direction.

CHAPTER IX.

NIX'S MATE, FORMERLY AN ISLAND. — GRANTED TO CAPTAIN JOHN GALLOP. — FORM AND CONSTRUCTION OF THE MONUMENT. — ORIGIN OF ITS NAME. — A PLACE OF EXECUTION FOR PIRATES. — EXECUTION OF WILLIAM FLY AND OTHERS. — GALLOP'S ISLAND. — GRANTED TO JOHN GALLOP. — PURCHASED BY THE CITY OF BOSTON. — FAMOUS PLACE FOR PLEASURE PARTIES. — OLD JOE SNOW. — RENDEZVOUS FOR SOLDIERS DURING THE CIVIL WAR. — USED FOR QUARANTINE.

After passing Long-Island light, and the beacon on the southerly end of Deer Island, the reader will come in sight of a peculiarly shaped monument, a tall pyramid upon a square stone base, the whole about thirty-two feet in height, and resting on what, at low tide, appears to be an extensive shoal covered with stones of a suitable size for ballast for vessels. This shoal, of about an acre in extent, is what remains of a once respectable island, as far as size is concerned; as may be seen by the following record made in 1636: —

"There is twelve acres of land granted to John Gallop, upon Nixes Iland, to enjoy to him & his heirs for ever, if the iland be so much."

NIX'S MATE.

There was once enough land on this island to answer for pasturage ground; and less than a hundred years back, the island was used for the purpose of grazing sheep. William Gallop was a noted pilot in his day, and was better acquainted with the harbor than any other man of his time. To his ability as a pilot and fisherman he added that of a good fighter; for on one occasion, when on a trading voyage to Block island, that lies off the coast of Rhode Island, he and his two young sons and boatman heroicically fought fourteen Indians on board a boat they had captured belonging to John Oldham of Boston, whom the Indians had killed. Gallop and his party killed all the Indians but one, whom he brought with him to Boston.

There is a story connected with this island, that the mate of a certain Captain Nix was executed upon it for the killing of his master; and that he, to the time of his death, insisted upon his innocence, and told the hangman, that, in proof of it, the island would be washed away.

The island was used for many years for the execution and burial of pirates, and an account of a case which happened many years ago may not be out of place in this connection. It is thus given in the Boston *News Letter*, published July 14, 1726: —

"On Tuesday the twelfth instant, about 3 P. M., were executed here for Piracy, Murder, &c., three of the condemned Persons mentioned in our last, viz., William Fly, Capt., Samuel Cole, Quartermaster, and Henry Greenville; the other viz. Gorge Condick, was Repreaved at the place of execution for a Twelve Month and a day, and is to be recommended to His Majesty's Grace and Favor. Fly behaved himself very unbecoming even to the last; however advised Masters of Vessels not to be severe and Barbarous to their Men, which might be a reason why so many turned Pirates; the other Two seem'd Penitent, beg'd that others might be warned by 'em. Their Bodies were carried in a Boat to a small Island call'd Nicks's-Mate, about 2 Leagues from the Town, where the abovesaid Fly was hung up in Irons, as a Spectacle for the Warning of others, especially Sea faring Men; the other Two were buried there."

The infamous notoriety which this island bore was equally shared in by other localities. Bird Island, the flats at the entrance of the Charles River, the Common, and the Neck are frequently alluded to as the places of execution and burial of criminals. John Quelch and his six companions in piracy were hung on June 13, 1704; Thomas Hawkins, a young man of the most respectable connections in the province, was executed, with his nine associates, Jan. 27, 1689. Samuel Bellamy and his six pirates paid their forfeit in May, 1717; and Archer and White were gibbeted on an island June 2, 1724, for piracy. Probably most of these pirates met their fate on this island, as it was the principal place in the harbor for the execution of pirates.

Southeast of Nix's Mate is Gallop's Island, which takes its name from Captain John Gallop, who was the first owner of the island, and also the proprietor of Nix's Mate; and at his death, in January, 1649, was valued at £15, and was estimated to contain sixteen acres, and was at a very early date under the jurisdiction of the town of Hull. The easterly part of the island is formed into a low Beachy Point, so called, being composed chiefly of small stones and gravel. This has always been noted as one of the most fertile of the islands in the harbor, and has from time immemorial been cultivated as a farm, in the days of the old quarantine regulations, the occupants supplying the vessels in the Hospital Roads with vegetables and milk, and pure water from a never-failing spring.

On the north side is a very abrupt and high bluff, surrounded by a sea wall. Upon the top of the bluff earth-works were thrown up during the Revolution for defensive purposes, which added to the discomfiture of the British after the evacuation of Boston.

In April, 1812, Mr. Caleb Rice of Hingham sold the island to Lemuel Brackett of Quincy for the sum of $1,630; in 1819, Peter Newcomb, the then tenant of the island, bought it for $1,815, and it was frequently called Newcomb's Island. Mr. Newcomb died in April, 1833, and was buried at Hull. The island was then occupied by the well-known "Joe Snow," and became a famous resort for pleasure parties, and his name will long be remembered by the numerous persons who have partaken of his good cheer and remarkable style of his hospitality.

Soon after the breaking-out of the Rebellion, the island was lent to the Government by the City of Boston, which purchased it in 1860 of Charles Newcomb for $6,500, and it was used as a rendezvous for enlisted soldiers, its green hill being covered with tents and barracks, and its turf trodden down, and its pleasant appearance almost blotted out. At the close of the war, the establishment at Gallop's Island became unnecessary, and the island was deserted by the soldiery, and the barracks consequently vacated, and the buildings turned over to the city, and the island was annexed to the quarantine establishment of the city, in view of the danger of a threatening infectious disease, which would require more than ordinary quarantine accommodation, and which fortunately was never put into use by the advent of the much-dreaded disease.

CHAPTER X.

LOVELL'S ISLAND. — ITS POSITION, FORM, AND SIZE. — THE GREAT ROCK AND ITS SAD HISTORY. — THE ISLAND GRANTED TO CHARLESTOWN IN 1636. — SOLD TO BOSTON IN 1782. — WRECK OF THE "MAGNIFIQUE." — THE MAN-OF-WAR "AMERICA." — GEORGE'S ISLAND FORMERLY PEMBERTON'S ISLAND. — BOUGHT BY BOSTON AND CONVEYED TO THE UNITED STATES. — DESCRIPTION OF FORT WARREN. — CONFINEMENT OF MASON AND SLIDELL IN SAME. — REBEL PRISONERS CONFINED THERE DURING THE REBELLION.

Northeast of Gallop's Island is situated Lovell's Island, which is about a third of a mile in width, and three-quarters of a mile in length. On the northerly point a sea-wall has been erected to prevent the washing away of this exposed part of the island. It contains one hill, with marshes to the north, east, and south, and several salt-water ponds. On the top of the hill may be seen, as the reader passes by the island, a large boulder, that has served for many generations as a comfortable cooking place. About fifty years ago, in mid-winter, in the dead of night, a coaster from Maine struck on Ram's Head, a shoal on its northerly point, causing immediate shipwreck; and, although the passengers, fifteen in number, succeeded in landing safely, and procuring shelter under the lee of the great rock, they all froze to death before morning, it being one of the coldest nights of the year, the thermometer being below zero. On the morning succeeding this dreadful event, the bodies were found closely huddled together in the eternal sleep of death. Two young persons, who were about to be married, and who were coming to Boston to make marriage purchases, were found dead beside the rock, locked in each others' arms. Few in their hilarious moments, under this friendly boulder, little dream of the agony of that awful night.

This island undoubtedly took its name from Captain William Lovell, who was of Dorchester in 1630. The first record to be found concerning the island is of October, 1636, in which the following record appears: —

"Lovel's Iland is granted to Charlestown provided they employ it for fishing by their own townsmen, or hinder not others."

Any one seeing the island now would hardly expect to find the following on the records: —

"The Iland called Lovel's Iland is given unto the inhabitants of Charles Towne & their heires and successors forever, pvided, that halfe of the timber & fire woode shall belong to the garrison at the Castle, to be impved wholly there."

There may be some person living that can remember the large tree that formerly stood at the south point of the island, as it was a mark used by all the pilots in the olden time in guiding them up the harbor. Similar trees, which have likewise disappeared, were preserved upon nearly all the islands for the same purpose.

In 1767, Charlestown sold the island "to Elisha Leavitt, of Hingham, for £266 13s. 4d., together with the dwelling-house and fences, etc." Mr. Leavitt left it in 1790 to his grandson, Caleb Rice; and from him it passed into the possession of the City of Boston in 1825, together with George's Island, both for the sum of $6,000; and the city conveyed it immediately to the Government for the same amount of money.

In 1782, a most unfortunate shipwreck occurred on this island.

Boston Harbor was frequented during the Revolutionary War by the naval forces of France, the ally of the Americans, for supplies and repairs. The Count D'Estaing was here in the fall of 1778; and a part of the fleet of the Count de Grasse, who landed Lafyette and the French army at Yorktown, came here in 1782, just after his unfortunate and unsuccessful attempt in the West Indies, where he was so completely and dreadfully defeated by the British. Admiral Vanbaird, with fourteen sail of this fleet, arrived in Boston Harbor August 11, 1782, being a division of the unfortunate fleet of the Count that escaped.

On entering the harbor through the Narrows, the pilot conducted the flag-ship, the "Magnifique," — as its name implied, a magnificent French seventy-four, — against the bar on Lovell's Island, and there it sank, and there its skeleton lies at the present day, imbedded in the sand.

Several attempts have been made to obtain treasure from this wreck, but they have not proved in any degree remunerative. One attempt, made about forty years ago, gave no return except specimens of very beautiful wood, of which the vessel was built. In July, 1859, another trial was equally unsuccessful, except in producing considerable quantities of copper, lead, and cannon-shot.

The French fleet left the harbor, and the pilot was transferred "up town" to become a sexton and undertaker, he having served a sufficient apprenticeship in burying; and it was no uncommon thing to find on a Sunday morning, chalked on the meeting-house door of the New North Church, the following inscription: —

> "*Don't run this ship ashore,*
> *As you did the seventy-four.*"

The loss of this French man-of-war was a serious matter for young America. Congress built a seventy-four-gun ship called the "America" at Portsmouth, the first line-of-battle ship ever built in America, and the command awarded to Commodore Paul Jones. This vessel was presented Louis XVI. to replace the lost "Magnifique." But it came finally to a poor market; for it was captured from the French by the English, and became a part of the great English navy.

The bar on the extreme westerly end of the island is called Man-of war Bar, on account of the loss of this vessel, and the sand and gravel

FORT WARREN.

has collected to such an extent around the wreck that a large portion of it has been converted into solid land, and the part in which the main part of the wreck of the ship is buried is now never overflowed at high water by ordinary tides.

During the operation of widening the main ship-channel on the southwest portion of the island in 1868, large pieces of planks and portions of massive oak timbers were struck at depths of twenty-one to twenty-five feet, and brought up by the machine; these were evidently fragments of the old seventy-four.

South of Lovell's Island lies George's Island, on which Fort Warren is situated. This island was early in the possession of James Pemberton of Hull, and called Pemberton's Island. It passed through various hands till it came into the possession of Caleb Rice, who sold it in 1825 to the City of Boston, when it was transferred to the United States. This island contains thirty-five acres, and the side exposed to the sea has been protected by a sea-wall, and a very strong fort named Fort Warren has been erected on it. Its walls are constructed of Quincy granite, nicely hammered, and the interior material for the foundation is composed of Cape-Ann granite. Over the entrance is the following inscription: "*Fort Warren, 1850.*"

This is not the first attempt at fortifying George's Island. In the autumn of the year of 1778, while the vessels of the Count D'Estaing were riding at Nantasket Roads, an earth-work was thrown up on the eastern side of the island, for the protection of vessels passing into the harbor against any attacks of the English cruisers which were then cruising in these waters.

At the early part of the war, the fort was used for rendezvous purposes, and some of the best regiments recruited in Massachusetts were thoroughly drilled within its walls before being sent into the field where they performed such distinguished service.

Mason and Slidell, the two Confederate commissioners, that were sent by the Confederate Government to represent the Southern Confederacy in England and France, and were taken out of the British mail steamer "Trent" by Captain Wilkes of the "San Jacinto," while *en route* from Havana to England, and which nearly embroiled this country in a war with England, were confined in Fort Warren until given up to the English Government.

During the war it was used as a prison for rebels. Only the most desperate, however, such as guerillas, and some of the most noted officers, whom the Government intended to keep during the war, and not exchange, were kept here; for the fort was too far from the seat of war to keep such prisoners as were intended to be quickly exchanged.

CHAPTER XI.

BUG LIGHT. — DESCRIPTION OF SAME. — RAINSFORD ISLAND. — ITS EARLY HISTORY. — REMOVAL OF THE QUARANTINE FROM SPECTACLE ISLAND TO RAINSFORD ISLAND. — LOCATION OF HOSPITALS. — OLD BURYING GROUND. — THE ISLAND NOW USED BY THE PAUPERS. — PETTICK'S ISLAND. — ITS FORM AND SIZE. — CREW OF A FRENCH TRADING-VESSEL MASSACRED THERE BY THE INDIANS. — THE VESSEL BURNT AND SOME OF THE CREW CARRIED INTO CAPTIVITY. — GREAT MORTALITY AMONG THE INDIANS SHORTLY AFTER.

After passing Fort Warren, an odd-looking structure will be seen to the northeast of it, and known as the Bug Light. It is on the extreme end of the spit or sand-bar stretching away from the Great Brewster, and is set up on iron stilts, presenting a very peculiar appearance. It has a fixed red light, and can be seen in pleasant weather about seven miles. The structure is painted of a dark red color, and its lantern is about thirty-five feet above the level of the sea. It was built in 1856, and is intended, when in range with Long-Island Light, to lead the mariner clear of Harding's Ledge, a most dangerous reef of rocks about two miles out at sea.

Southeast of Fort Warren lies Rainsford's Island, sometimes called Hospital or Quarantine Island. It is about half a mile in length from east to west, and very narrow for its length, and is supposed to contain about eleven acres of ground. Its North Bluff, so called, where is situated the chief part of the land which is in any degree supplied with available soil, is quite elevated, being about thirty-five feet above high-

RAINSFORD'S ISLAND.

water mark. At the western extremity is a prominent point of land called Small-Pox Point, from the fact that for many years the Small-Pox Hospital was situated on it.

The first known owner of this Island was Edward Rainsford, who was supposed to be of the town of Hull, and was sent over here by Mr. Owen Rowe, a wealthy London tradesman, who wrote to Governor Winthrop in 1635, requesting that "Mr. Rainsford may be accommodated with lands for a farme to keepe my cattcle, that so my stocks may be preserved."

The chief use of the island was for the pasturage of cattle; and, as Elder Rainsford had charge of those sent over by Mr. Rowe, it is supposed that he obtained a grant of the island for that purpose.

The island passed through various hands till 1736, when it was purchased by the colony for the sum of £570, to be used for the purpose of "building a suitable and convenient House on Rainsford Island, lying between Long Island and the Maine Land near the town of Hull, to be used and improved as a publick hospital for the reception and accommodation of such sick and infectious persons as shall be sent there by order."

In a preceding chapter on Spectacle Island an account was given of the first Quarantine started by the town of Boston on that island.

After nearly twenty years' use of that locality, there was a feeling in the community that the right place had not been selected. Spectacle Island was too near the town, and was among other occupied islands. It had no good road near it for the anchorage of detained vessels, and was also suitable for pasturage, containing as it did about sixty acres of good grass land. This, therefore, was the reason for transferring the hospital to Rainsford Island.

The present quarantine ground is near Deer Island, and also extends so as to include Gallop's Island. On the Great Head, upon the easterly part of North Bluff, as it is called, is situated an airy-looking house, which in recent years has been occupied by the superintendent of the institution. West of this are two buildings, the most southerly of which was built in 1819, and is designated as the Old Hospital, the Mansion House of quarantine days; while that just north of it is known as the New Female Hospital. A short distance toward the wharf is a smaller building known as the Cottage. Not far from this, and projecting southerly, is a long wharf, the ordinary means of approaching the island and its institutions.

After passing the narrow neck or beach, and upon what is called West Head, is a pretentious-looking building resembling a Grecian temple. West of this is the burial ground, in which are many stones, which, if they could speak, would tell strange stories. Some of them date back more than a hundred years. The remains of many of the old keepers of the island remain there in quiet slumber. The days are past, but not out of remembrance, when persons afflicted with several of the most loathsome infectious diseases were sent to the "island," almost certainly to die. The enlightenment of the present day, however, forbids all such outrages.

The island is occupied now mostly by paupers, and a new house on the northwesterly side of the island has been recently erected for their accommodation. Rainsford Island, with its variety of handsome substantial buildings, and its hills, rocks, and beaches, trees and shrubbery, presents one of the most attractive features of the harbor.

South of Fort Warren, and separated from the main-land by Hull Gut, is situated Pettick's Island, about a mile long and an average width of about a quarter of a mile. The island is divided into two hills called the East and West Heads, between which there is a smaller hill, and just south of this there is an island bluff called Prince's Head.

The earliest information we have concerning this island is from

FARM HOUSE, PETTICK'S ISLAND.

Morton of Ma-re Mount, who obtained some important facts from the Indians, who informed him that, previous to the arrival of any of the English, a French ship came into the harbor to trade, and while lying at anchor by an island, afterward called Pettick's Island, the Indians set upon the men at a disadvantage, killed many of them, and burnt the ship. The captives they distributed among five sachems of different tribes.

This statement agrees with what Dr. Mather afterward relates of the same tragedy. His informant gave him the name of the Frenchman living in his time, which was *Monsieur Finch*. The Indians treated their prisoners in a barbarous manner, and eventually killed them all but three or four. These they sent as curiosities about the country from one sachem to another. Some years after, when Captain Dermer was at Cape Cod, he found two of them alive, whom he redeemed out of their hands. When the English inquired of them why they had killed the Frenchmen, they justified themselves on some frivolous grounds; and, when they were told that the great God was angry with them, they looked significantly at one another, and inquired sneeringly of the English if they thought they were such fools as to believe that God could kill all the Indians.

Immediately after the Indians so cruelly treated the French sailors, a deadly sickness, supposed to be the small-pox, broke out among the Indians, which, as old authors say, caused them "to die in heaps all up and down the country, insomuch that the living were in no wise able to bury the dead." This the Indians considered a retribution on them for their wickedness.

Pettick's Island was granted to Charlestown in 1634 for twenty-one years, for the yearly rent of twenty shillings. In 1635 the rent was reduced to twelve pence. Before the lease expired, the town of Nantasket or Hull was commenced, and the island confirmed to it, and divided into lots of four acres each, and given to those who took two-acre lots at Hull. This island has always from that time been kept as private property.

In 1684 the Indian Josiah relinquished all his claim to the estate in the right of his father and grandfather.

A pilot for the various approaches to Weymouth and Hingham resides on the east side of the island opposite Hull, whose farm-buildings, orchard, and so forth, are nestled in the valley between the two great hills, presenting a very cheerful, home-like appearance.

CHAPTER XII.

HULL VISITED BY EARLY NAVIGATORS. — POINT ALLERTON AND ITS MONUMENT. — DESCRIPTION OF SHEEP ISLAND. — PUMPKIN ISLAND GRANTED TO WEYMOUTH. — SAMUEL WARD LEAVES IT TO HARVARD COLLEGE. — WHITE HEAD. — WORLD'S END. — DESCRIPTION OF WEIR RIVER. — COHASSET ROCKS. — NANTASKET BEACH. — DESCRIPTION OF WRECKS ON SAME DURING THE WINTER SEASON.

To the eastward of Pettick's Island, situated on the extreme end of the main-land, is the town of Hull, separated from Pettick's Island by "Hull Gut," through which flows the waters that form the southeast part of the harbor, creating a very strong current, and, when the tide and wind are in opposite directions, making considerable of a sea.

On the north of Hull will be noticed, at the end of the bar that makes out in the direction of Boston Light, a monument of a pyramid shape; this is on the end of Point Allerton, which has its Great Hill and Little Hill. At the end of the latter is the monument.

Frequent allusions have been made in these pages to Nantasket and Point Allerton, both of which are included in the town of Hull. Point Allerton is supposed to be the place visited by the Northmen in 1004, and described by them as an "abrupt promontory, well covered with forest trees," and named by them Krossaness; and also the place on which Myles Standish and his party landed when they explored Boston Harbor, in 1621, and found there lobsters which had been gathered by the Indians, and met a woman coming for them, and "contented" her for them. At this Place Captain Squib put ashore the colonist that settled Dorchester, in the year 1636. A part of them went and explored the Charles River up as far as Watertown in a boat they secured of an old planter; and the remainder went around by land till they came to Dorchester, where they decided to settle.

Hull was evidently settled by traders before the arrival of Winthrop's colony, and is the smallest town in the New-England States. The inhabitants mostly obtain their living by fishing, and of late years many fine residences have been erected here, which are occupied in the summer season by pleasure-seekers, and the town is fast becoming famous as a healthy, cool location for summer residences.

Hull is reached by the steamers of the Boston and Hingham Steamboat Company, and is the first place touched at after leaving Rowe's Wharf.

The steamer, again procceding on her course in a southeasterly direction, will next come to Sheep Island, anciently known as Sun Island. It contains but two acres, and must have been a poor place to keep sheep, although in the olden time it was valued for that purpose. The surface of the island is but a few feet above the water, and is fast washing away.

To the eastward of Sheep Island is Pumpkin Island, sometimes called Bumpkin Island. It contains about fifty acres of good pasture-land, and is beautifully situated in Hull shoals. The island was granted to the town of Weymouth in 1636, and in course of time this beautiful island is found in the possession of Mr. Samuel Ward, who in early colony days was a great land-owner; and by his will, executed in 1681, he bequeathed the island to Harvard College, in the following words : —

"The Island that I have given to the Colidge, which Lyeth Betwixte hingham and hull called Bomkin Island; my mind is that it shall be, and Remain for eveer, to harford Coledge, in newengland : the Rentt of itt to be for the easmentt of the charges of the Diatte of the Stu danttse that are in commonse."

The island is now valued at about twelve hundred dollars, and produces an income of about fifty dollars a year. In former years there was a farm-house on the island; but now it is uninhabited.

VIEW OF HULL.

The ruins of the cellar can be seen on the south side of the island, as well as the remains of an old wharf or landing; a well of good water, which is often used by camping-parties, can be found quite near the old landing. Several stone walls will also be observed crossing the island, all of which show that, at one time, the island was probably well farmed.

After passing Pumpkin Island, and continuing in a southeasterly course, we reach the entrance to Weir River. The neck of land on the left hand, on entering the river, is known as White Head; and the curious round peninsula attached by a slender bar to Planter's Hill, on the right hand, is World's End, and is situated in the town of Hingham. The scenery in this river is very beautiful, some portions of it bordered with grand cliffs, and some little distance up the river both shores are clothed with forests with scarcely a sign of human habitation. In fact, a person might imagine himself a hundred miles away from Boston, as far as any appearance of civilization is concerned; and yet it is less than an hour's sail. This is one of the most favorite resorts in the harbor

NANTASKET BEACH.

for camping parties, many persons staying here nearly the whole summer, camping in tents in the woods. One arm of the river approaches quite near the ocean, only a narrow strip of beach — the famous Nantasket — keeping it from entering the river.

Here is built the steamboat wharf, and is the end of the route of the Nantasket steamers. Many fine hotels are erected on the beach, and also extending in a southeasterly direction along the Cohasset shore are many fine hotels and summer residences away up on the rocks. This is the commencement of that "stern and rock-bound coast" which surrounds nearly all of Massachusetts Bay. Along the verge of the cliffs the sea dashes the surf frequently over the buildings, drenching them, and for an instant showing in the sun the fleeting hues of the rainbow. Now and then, when standing on the brink of some table-rock, the

BLACK ROCK.

plunge of a billow underneath causes a sensible tremor. A rock projecting out into the ocean, and known as Black Rock, presents a grand sight during a northeasterly storm; the sea breaking completely over it, and drenching it with spray.

In a northerly direction is Nantasket Beach, five miles long, of hard, smooth sand, the finest beach in New England. Surf-bathing and driving can be enjoyed on the beach, and lovers of natural scenery will find much to amuse and interest them; the numerous Hotels and Restaurants scattered along the shore offering ample refreshments for the inner man.

In many places along the beach timbers of wrecked vessels are met with, deeply bedded in the sand, the ribs of which, projecting out of the

WRECK ON NANTASKET BEACH.

sand, have the appearance of formidable teeth belonging to some sea monster.

During the winter season, many wrecks occur on this beach. Vessels on entering Boston Harbor mistake their bearings on dark nights, or are driven, in cold, blinding snow-storms, on to this inhospitable shore, and many lives and much property are lost yearly. In Hull, a number of signs, the names of various vessels cast ashore here during the past few years, may be observed nailed around the music stand in the centre of the town.

For a number of years the people of Hull bore rather a hard name, on account of their wrecking propensities; for many of them recognized the truth of the old saying, that "it is an ill wind that blows no one any good." Many readers will probably remember of the wreck of the bark "Kadosh" which took place here a few years ago, in which many lives were lost.

WRECK OF THE "KADOSH."

This chapter completes the first and most important route down the harbor. All the islands and points of interest described in previous chapters can be seen on this route by taking the Nantasket and Hull Steamer of the Hingham Steamboat Company, at Rowe's Wharf, Atlantic Avenue.

Another line of boats belonging to the same company, and stopping at Downer Landing and Hingham, will be described in route No. 2, in the next chapter.

CHAPTER XIII.

ROUTE SECOND. — FROM ROWE'S WHARF TO HINGHAM. — DESCRIPTION OF DOWNER LANDING, FORMERLY CROW POINT. — A FAMOUS RESORT FOR EXCURSIONISTS. — MELVILLE GARDEN. — ROSE STANDISH HOUSE. — RAGGED ISLAND. — WALTON GROVE. — VARIOUS ATTRACTIONS OF THE PLACE. — HINGHAM, AND ITS HARBOR AND ISLANDS. — THE OLD MEETING-HOUSE ERECTED IN 1681. — LAST RESTING-PLACE OF GOV. ANDREW. — DESCRIPTION OF THE TOWN.

The Boston and Hingham steamboats, starting from Rowe's Wharf, pursue the same course as the other steamers of the same line that run to Nantasket Beach, as described in the previous chapter, till they reach Pumpkin Island, or about off the entrance to Weir River, when they continue on to the south, and in a short time reach Downer Landing, formerly called Crow Point.

A few years ago, Mr. Downer, the well-known refiner of kerosene oil, bought the point, intending to improve it, and make a summer resort of it for himself and friends; but soon the beauties of the place became known, and he opened the grounds to the public, and it is now one of the finest pleasure resorts in New England. The grounds of the garden cover over ten acres, and here can be found every variety of amusement for picnic parties and daily excursionists, such as bowling and shooting alleys, swings, tilts, flying horses, and so forth. A large, handsome, and commodious hotel, the "Rose Standish House," and an excellent restaurant and music hall, row-boats, yachts with reliable skippers, a Punch and Judy show, and monkey cage containing every con-

DOWNER LANDING.

ceivable species of monkeys, clam-bakes, a large camera obscura, and many other things too numerous too mention, are among the attractions of this place.

The gardens are open every evening except Monday, and are illuminated with twenty Electric lights. Patrons can dance or listen to the music of Edmands' Band, day and evening.

Ragged Island, a small rocky island a short distance from Melville Garden, is connected with it by a ferry-boat which makes frequent trips to and from this beautiful and romantic island. The island has every convenience for picnic parties, such as shades, pavilions, and restaurants. A bridge from the garden connects it with a beautiful grove of ten acres, abounding in rocks and glens, and including a beautiful sheet of water which was made by a dam across Walton Cove, and what was formerly mud flats is now changed into a beautiful lake.

Mr. Downer, who has given his own name to the place, has expended a large fortune in laying out the grounds, and in executing his plans for making them the most desirable spot to be found in the harbor, thereby realizing almost the ideal of an elysian field for the tourist or pleasure-seeker. How well he has succeeded after many years of laborious toil must be left to the verdict of the visitor.

Pursuing a course due south, and passing the strait between Crow Point, now Downer Landing, on the west, and Planter's Hill on the east, the tourist will enter Hingham Harbor, and will notice first Button Island, then Ragged Island with the pavilion on it, and next Sarah and Langley Island, after which he will soon reach the steamboat wharf, and will have arrived in the town of Hingham, one of the oldest and wealthiest towns in the State, and noted for its beautiful scenery and pleasant drives, through its tree-lined streets and woodland roads. The old meeting-house, erected in 1681, is the oldest meeting-house in New England, and is in a good state of preservation, and good for some hundred of years yet to come.

In the cemetery connected with it rest the remains of the late John A. Andrew, the "War Governor of Massachusetts," to whose memory an elegant marble statue has been erected. A simple monument marks the resting-place of Major-General Benjamin Lincoln of Revolutionary fame, in the same cemetery.

Hingham was once noted for its fishing business; but now the wharves are deserted. Later it was well known for its manufacture of woodenware; but at the present time but little is doing in that business. Hingham at present resembles an old wealthy English country town. The old inhabitants are very conservative, and are living on the fruits of past labor, and taking life easily in their beautiful town.

RAGGED ISLAND.

CHAPTER XIV.

ROUTE THIRD: FROM INDIA WHARF TO NAHANT. — POINT SHIRLEY, FORMERLY PULLING POINT. — THE DERIVATION OF THE NAME. — CAPTAIN MUGFORD. — REMARKABLE EXPLOIT THERE DURING THE REVOLUTIONARY WAR. — CUTTING OUT THE POWDER SHIP. — FIGHT IN SHIRLEY GUT, AND DEATH OF CAPTAIN MUGFORD. — NAHANT BOUGHT OF BLACK WILLIAM, THE INDIAN CHIEF. — THE FORESTS DESTROYED. — INFESTED WITH WOLVES, BEARS, AND WILD BEASTS. — DESCRIPTION AND EARLY HISTORY.

Leaving the foot of India Wharf by way of the Nahant steamer, the reader will proceed down the harbor, pursuing the same course as described in Route 1, till opposite Governor's Island, when the steamer will proceed in a northeasterly direction, passing very near to Apple Island, and between Point Shirley, formerly called Pulling Point, and Deer Island, through the passage known as "Shirley Gut." In reference to the derivation of the name of Pulling Point, the following old account says: "Pulling-Point is so called because the boats are by the seasings or roads haled against the tide which is very strong, it is the usual channel for boats to pass into Mattachusets Bay." It was called Point Shirley in 1753, in honor of Governor Shirley.

During the blockade of Boston in the time of the Revolutionary War, Captain James Mugford, of Marblehead, earned for himself at this spot a brief glory and most pathetic fame. He had been impressed on board of the British frigate "Lively" in Marblehead Harbor. His wife went aboard of the frigate, and, stating that they had just been married, demanded his release, which soon after was granted, but not before he had heard the sailors talking about a "powder ship" which they were expecting from England. Resolving to capture her, he applied for a commission, but sailed before it came, thereby rendering himself and crew liable to be hung as pirates if captured. He sailed in a small fishing smack with twenty men. After lying in wait for some time, the vessel was seen approaching Boston Harbor. The men were sent below, where they were crowded into the cuddy; and the store-ship, not expecting an enemy in the peaceful-appearing fisherman, with only a few men on deck, allowed her to approach quite close, when Mugford and his men grappled with her, and the men, crowding out of the hold, boarded her, and captured her in sight of the whole British fleet, and carried her safely into Boston, at a time when Washington's stock of powder did not amount to more than nine rounds per man. If the vessel had been loaded with gold, it would not have been so valuable to the American army as this powder-ship.

A few days after, waiting his opportunity to return to Marblehead without being observed by the British fleet, he sailed by way of Shirley Gut, but was cut off by a swarm of boats from the British fleet then lying in Nantasket Roads. The fight was desperate, and in a hand-to-hand encounter Captain Mugford was killed while attempting to keep off the boarders. But his vessel got away safely through the Gut, bearing his lifeless body to Marblehead, where a few days later the marine regiment of which he was captain buried it with solemn pomp.

After passing through Shirley Gut, the reader will be outside of the harbor and in Massachusetts Bay. A few miles' sailing in a northeasterly direction, and Nahant is reached; and, although not strictly coming within a history of Boston Harbor, yet as it is easily reached from the city by steamers, and contains many points of interest, we will give a brief description of it in this chapter.

Nahant belonged to the Indians for many years after the settlement of Salem and Lynn by the English. The name is said to signify, in the Indian language, an "island." It was purchased of the Indians by Farmer Dexter — who was the first land speculator of Nahant — in 1630 for a suit of clothes, and was afterward again sold for "two pestle-stones." The original owner was an Indian chief named by the whites

NAHANT ROCKS.

"Black Will," who was cruelly killed at Richman Island, Scarborough, Me., in revenge for the murder of Walter Bagnall, who was killed by Indians in 1631. Black Will was hung unjustly, for he did not take any part in the murder; and, if he had, Gov. Winthrop says Bagnall was "a wicked fellow, and had much wronged the Indians." It seems that Farmer Dexter was not allowed to obtain possession of his purchase, for the town contested the title, yet it seems clear from the depositions that he really bought it of Black Will, or Duke Will, as he was sometimes called. The case was tried in court, and William Witter, farmer, testified as follows: —

"Black will or duke william so called came to my house (which was two or three miles from Nahant), when Thomas Dexter had bought Nahant for a suit of clothes, the said Black will Asked me what I would give him for the Land my house stood vppon it being his land, and his ffather's wigwame stood thereabouts. James Saggamore, being a youth was present, all of them acknowledging Blacke will to be the right owner of the Land my house stood on and Sagamore Hill and Nahant was his. He bought Nahant and Sagomer Hill and Swampscoate of Black William for two pestle-stones."

Nahant was used as a pasturage for cattle, many of the settlers even bringing their cattle from Salem. The place was well wooded, but was robbed of its wood, as the islands in Boston Harbor were,—for firewood; and when the peninsula was divided into lots in 1656, it was voted "that every person should clear his lot of wood in 6 years and he or they that do not clear their lotts of wood shall pay fifty shillings for the townes use."

Efforts have been made of late years to rear trees of every description on Nahant, which so far, except in a few cases, have been unsuccessful; the young trees are probably killed by the salt-water spray blown over them during severe storms. In the storms the waves dash over the highest rocks around the shore. It is probable that trees of various kinds will flourish here as buildings multiply to break off the wind, and afford them shelter.

The wolves, bears, and other wild beasts abounded here in such quantities that the train-band or militia were marched there in a body in 1634 to hunt wolves; but the wolves have all disappeared from Nahant,

VIEW OF NAHANT.

and the Indians are all gone, the trees cut down, and from the rudest spot of a rude people, it has become the resort of the most fashionable. Its broad and extensive beaches, its rugged, rock-bound shores, its natural curiosities, such as the Pulpit Rock, Spouting Horn, Swallow's Cave, the fishing, gunning, bathing, riding, and other amusements, all have their attraction, and by going to Nahant for a day can be seen and enjoyed. Hot as it is in the city, here you may ride, bathe, or fish in the day, and be sure of a good, cool, comfortable night's sleep afterward. The name and fame of Nahant have been rehearsed and sung in prose and poetry, and its rocks and beaches have been the theme of the historian and the subject of the painter; and yet not half has been said, sung, or painted, and in the limited space of this small volume we can give only such facts as we may be able to gather in relation to its early history and present appearance.

The Indian enjoyed it in all its natural beauty and freshness. We enjoy it shorn of much of its original beauty, but unimpaired in its solid and sublime grandeur.

Nahant is a peninsula extending into the ocean, the shore is entirely rock-bound, and connected with the main-land by a beach three miles long of hard, smooth sand.

About a mile from Nahant along the beach is Little Nahant, containing about fifty acres. On Great Nahant are the village cottages, church, hotels, steamboat landing, and so forth.

CHAPTER XV,

ROUTE FOURTH. — FOSTER'S WHARF, LONG ISLAND, AND LOVELL'S GROVE. — THE WEST WAY. — MOON HEAD. — TO BE USED FOR THE TERMINUS TO THE SEWER. — THE INJURY IT WILL CAUSE THE HARBOR. — HANGMAN'S ISLAND USED BY LOBSTER FISHERMEN. — NUT ISLAND. — HOUGH'S NECK. — GRAPE ISLAND. — INDIAN RELICS RECENTLY DISCOVERED THERE. — BRITISH FORAGING PARTIES VISIT THE ISLAND. — FRIGHT OF THE INHABITANTS OF WEYMOUTH. — THE ISLAND INHABITED AT PRESENT BY AN OLD SLAVER. — REMARKABLE LIFE AND ADVENTURES OF SAME.

Proceeding down the harbor by way of the steamboat of the Boston Bay Steamboat Company, we go over the same course as described in Route 1, as far as Long Island, where the steamboat makes a landing. Then, pursuing a southwesterly course between Spectacle Island and Long Island to what is known as the West Way or Back Way, the reader will come to Moon Head or Moon Island, one of the most marked objects in the harbor, on account of the high bluff which it presents on its northerly side. It is connected at low water with Squantum by a bar over which the cattle walk to the island. It has been used from time immemorial for pasturage, and is a famous spot for excursion parties to land for cooking and camping purposes. Clams in great abundance and of delicious flavor can be obtained by digging on the bar.

But this island is soon to be put to a different use, which will forever put a stop to its being used for the above purposes. The reservoir of the new sewer now in process of construction is intended to be built on this island, where all the sewage of Boston will be pumped, and emptied into the waters of the harbor, to fill up its channels and line its shores with filth. The clear blue waters of Quincy Bay will be contaminated and forsaken by the lobsters and fish with which it now abounds; the seals will no longer sport on its rocks, or its waters be sought in the fall of the year by the wild fowl. This beautiful bay, instead of being known by its pure water and air, will become as well known as Miller's River, the Back Bay, or the Roxbury canal were before their filthy waters were filled in; a place that will be forsaken alike both by man and the fowls of the air and the fishes of the sea; and from being one of the healthiest spots in the vicinity of Boston it will become as unhealthy and pestiferous as the swamps and bayous of Louisiana.

It seems a strange fact that a city having the reputation that Boston has for its wealth and intelligence should not be guided by its former experience, and also that of other large cities, such as London and Paris, and utilize its sewage, and return it to the soil whence it came; for Massachusetts, with its sterile soil, can ill afford to lose that matter which would make a desert bloom. Neither can Boston afford to have its air contaminated or its channels filled up, for the waters of the harbor are not too deep as they are now. This sewage business savors too much of a job; and, if Boston is not careful, it may suffer as much financially as it will in its salubrity, for here will be established an invitation to all the different contagious diseases that have afflicted the southern coasts to visit this now healthy region. And this all caused through the ignorance of our city officials, and cupidity of a few unscrupulous politicians. May the day be far distant before Moon Head and Quincy Bay are contaminated with this sewage, is the earnest prayer of the writer and all lovers of natural beauty and of Boston Harbor in particular.

When near Moon Head, a view can be had of Squantum, and also the west side of Long Island, Rainsford Island, and Pettick's Island, all described in Route 1.

Passing Moon Head, the tourist enters Quincy Bay, the largest extent of water in Boston Harbor. It contains but few islands, and is nearly four miles across in each direction. Nearly in the centre of the bay is a small rocky island with a shanty on it; the island is known as Hangman's Island, probably on account of its being used in olden times for the purpose of hanging pirates on, as many other islands were. The

HANGMAN'S ISLAND, QUINCY BAY.

island is now inhabited during the summer season by several men engaged in lobster-fishing, who can be seen at all times in different parts of the bay, hauling up their lobster-pots. Numerous seals can be seen sporting about the rocks in this bay, which seems to be a favorable place for them; and in the fall of the year it is the resort of ducks, coot, and other wild fowl.

South of Pettick's Island is Nut Island, containing about six acres, connected by a bar with Hough's Neck, on which is Quincy Great Hill.

Nut Island has been used recently by the United-States Government for the purpose of testing ordnance, under the supervision of Wiard; these fruitless experiments have cost the Government upward of half a million dollars. A few years ago a camping party attempting to cross to the island, with a horse and wagon over the bar, at high water, the team was capsized, and several persons drowned.

LOBSTER-FISHERMAN.

Continuing on in an easterly direction the tourist will come to Grape Island, which is between the entrance of Weymouth Fore River and Weymouth Back River. It contains fifty acres, and has two hills. A few weeks after the battle of Lexington, three sloops and a cutter came down from Boston, and anchored off the mouth of Fore River. The people of Weymouth were greatly alarmed. A landing was momentarily expected, and three hundred soldiers were reported marching on the town. Three alarm guns were fired, the bells rung, and the drum beat to arms, the alarm and confusion being very great. Every house below North Weymouth was deserted by the women and children. The minute-men poured in rapidly from Hingham, Randolph, and Braintree, and all the neighboring towns, till nearly two thousand of them were on the ground. Then it was discovered that the enemy were foraging, and engaged in removing hay from Grape Island. By this time they had secured about three tons. The minute-men had brought a sloop and lighter around from Hingham, on which they put out for the island, whereupon the enemy decamped, and no one was hurt.

On another occasion, a few months later, Captain Goold of Weymouth, with twenty-five men, went out from Moon Head, and crossed over to Long Island, and burned a house and a barn full of hay. On this occasion they had a sharp skirmish, for the British men-of-war sent out their cutter to intercept the party. They all, however, got back safely, except one man of the covering force on Moon Head, who was killed by a cannon-ball.

Grape Island has been inhabited from the first settlement of the harbor, and used for fishing and farming purposes. The house now on the island is situated in a valley between two hills, near to deep water, where there is a good landing, and near a spring of fresh water. A short distance to the westward, on the bar, clams can be found in abundance. This must have been a favorite place of resort for the Indians, for the writer visited the island a short time ago, and obtained there three stone tomahawks or celts, that were used by the Indians. They were found in the rear of the house, in the garden, which is composed almost wholly of shells, resembling somewhat the shell-heaps of Florida. Captain Smith, the occupant of the house, has just removed about fifteen tons of stone from the garden. They were about a foot beneath the soil, and set up edgewise, forming a circle, the bottom covered with beach gravel. Here the Indians built their fires till the stones were hot, then withdrew the fire, and placed the clams, lobsters, and corn, on which wet seaweed was piled. The result was a delicious clam-bake. Quite a number of such places were found close together, and here were found the stone tomahawks.

Captain Smith lives on the island all alone summer and winter, and lives on clams, lobsters, fish, and what little vegetables he can raise, and for 50 cents he will boil you a bucketful of clams. A few years ago it was stated in the papers that he had died during the winter and his remains were eaten up by the rats, but the old man is good for some winters yet to come.

This island takes its name from the fact that probably grapes abounded on it once when it was wooded, for considerable quantities are found yet ashore on the main-land but a short distance from the island, where there is the most beautiful woods in the harbor, affording a grateful shade to camping and excursion parties. The island is situated at the entrance to Weymouth Back River, and the woods are on the east side of the river and extend back as far as Downer Landing, from which place the river can be reached, as that is the nearest place the steamer comes to Back River. The only direct way to reach the river is by yachts.

This island was bought some years since by Mr. Samuel Litchfield, for $6,000, and is used for pasturing sheep and horses.

CHAPTER XVI.

WEYMOUTH FORE RIVER. — CALLED WESSAGUSSET. — SETTLED BY WESTON'S COLONY IN 1622. — ARE IN A STARVING CONDITION. — THEY SEEK HELP FROM PLYMOUTH. — ROBBING THE INDIANS. — ONE OF THEIR NUMBER HUNG. — MASSACRE OF THE INDIANS BY MYLES STANDISH. — THE COLONY IS ABANDONED. — RACCOON ISLAND. — LOVELL'S GROVE. — ITS ATTRACTIONS TO EXCURSIONISTS.

The steamboat, passing to the westward of Grape Island, will enter Weymouth Fore River, the place of the earliest settlement made in Boston Harbor, by Mr. Thomas Weston, and was called by the Indians Wessagusset.

In 1622, Mr. Thomas Weston, a London merchant, sent over two vessels under the charge of his brother-in-law, Richard Greene. They were named the "Charity," of one hundred tons; and the "Swan," of thirty. The colony was made up of the roughest material, picked up in the streets and docks of London; among them was one surgeon, Mr. Salisbury, and a lawyer from Furnivall's Inn, afterward notoriously known as Thomas Morton of Merry Mount. Such as they were, however, they safely landed at Plymouth toward the end of June, — some sixty stout fellows, without the remotest idea why they had come, or what they had come to do. The old settlers did not look upon them as a very desirable accession to the colony, especially as they early evinced a disinclination to honest labor, and a well-developed appetite for green corn.

It was August before the party reached Wessagusset, and they selected for their permament quarters the south shore of the Fore River. The larger ship, the "Charity," returned to England; and the smaller one, the "Swan," remained for the use of the settlement. Enough supplies were left to last during the winter; but, as they were a wasteful, improvident set, they squandered most of their resources before the winter was begun, and, with their trading with the Indians, ruined the market, giving for a quart of corn what before would have bought a beaver-skin, thus occasioning complaints by the prudent Plymouth settlers.

At the beginning of New Years, the colony found itself face to face with dire want. The hungry settlers bartered every thing they had with the Indians, even to the clothes on their backs, and the blankets from their beds, in exchange for food. They made canoes for the Indians, and for a mere pittance of corn became their hewers of wood and drawers of water, thus making the fatal mistake of degrading themselves before the Indians.

During that long, dreary winter, they must have wished themselves back in the slums of London. The cold tide ebbed and flowed before their rude block-house, the frost was in the ground, and the snow was on it. Their ammunition was nearly exhausted, so that they could not kill game. They searched the woods for nuts, and followed out the tide, digging for clams. One poor fellow, in grubbing along the shore for shell-fish, sank into the mud, and, being weak, could not drag himself out, and was found there dead. In all, ten perished.

The settlers alternately cringed before the Indians, and abused them; and they, seeing them so poor and weak and helpless, first grew to despise and then to oppress them. Naturally starving men of their description had recourse to theft, and there was no one to steal from but the Indians; so the Indians found their hidden stores of corn disturbed, and knew just where to look for the thieves. This led to a bitter feeling among the Indians. The Indians would not lend or sell them any food; for they did not have any to spare.

Finally the settlers thought of having recourse to violence. They sent a letter by an Indian messenger to the Plymonth people requesting them to assist them in taking from the Indians what was necessary by force; but the Plymouth magistrates would not countenance any such proceeding, neither could they send them any food, but advised them to worry through the winter, and live on nuts and shell-fish, as they themselves were doing, especially as they enjoyed the additional advantage of having an oyster-bed, which the people of Plymouth had not.

Meanwhile they continued robbing the Indians, who retaliated by treating the poor wretches like dogs, and threatened to treat them as they did the unfortunate Frenchmen a few years before, whose vessel they destroyed on Pettick's Island, and killed and made captives of the crew, whose knives and arms they displayed.

Finally one unfortunate and skillful thief was detected, and bitter complaint made against him. The terror-stricken settlers offered to give him up to the savages to be dealt with as they saw fit; but the sachem replied, "Do justice upon him yourselves, and let your neighbors do justice upon theirs," and then left the place indignantly, and the settlers, in their alarm, took the thief, and executed him in the presence of the Indians.

But accounts differ as to whom they hung. Some say that the thief was an able-bodied man, whom they could ill afford to spare; that "he would stand them in some good steede, being younge and stronge, fit for resistance against an enemy;" and that "he was an able-bodied man that ranged the woodes to see what it would afford, he lighted by accident on an Indian barne and from thence did take a capful of corne." "And as they did all agree that one must die and one shall die this young mans clothes we will take off and put upon one that is old and impotent, a sickly person that cannot escape death that die hee must, put the young mans clothes on this man, and let the sick person be hanged in the other steede." And so the Weymouth hanging passed into history, and was accepted as historical truth.

So through the hard, long, savage winter, those seventy poor hungry wretches shivered around their desolate habitations, or straggled about among the neighboring wigwams, in search of food. Meantime the depredations still went on, and the Indians grew more and more aggressive, and were now watching the Wessagusset settlement very closely, and were determined to rid themselves of their unwelcome neighbors. The settlers still, however, lived on in their reckless way, mixing freely with the savages, and taking no precaution against surprise; but one of their number was alarmed, and very early one morning, preparing a small pack, he took a hoe in his hand, and left the settlement as if in search of nuts or about to dig shell-fish, and, when unobserved by the Indians, plunged into the swamp, and began to make his way, thinly clothed and half starved, and without even a compass, in the direction of Plymouth, and soon after reached the settlement, exhausted but in safety.

The next day, Myles Standish, with a little army of eight men, set sail, and reached the Fore River on the day following; and steered directly for the "Swan," which was lying at her moorings. Greatly to his surprise he found her wholly deserted. A musket was fired, which attracted the attention of a few miserable wretches busy searching for nuts. Standish landed, and after some conversation with some of the principal men, promptly began his preparations to cruelly massacre the Indians.

After an interview with their chief Pecksuot, plans were made to treacherously get all the Indians he could into his power, and then to kill them in cold blood. He accordingly invited them to meet him the next day inside of his stockade, which the Indians did, they not suspecting treachery. Two of the chiefs, Pecksuot and Wituwamat, and two other of the principal Indians, met Standish and several of his men in a room, where they had a talk. Suddenly Standish gave the signal, and flung himself on Pecksuot, snatching his knife from his sheath on his neck, and stabbing him with it. The door was closed, and a life-and-death struggle ensued. The Indians were taken by surprise; but they fought hard, making little noise, but catching at their weapons, and struggling until they were cut almost to pieces.

Finally Pecksuot, Wituwamat, and a third Indian were killed; while a fourth, a youth of eighteen, was overpowered and secured, whom Standish subsequently hung.

There were eight warriors inside the stockade. Standish and his party killed four, and secured one, and Weston's people dispatched two more. One only escaped to give the alarm, which was rapidly spread through the Indian village.

Standish immediately followed up his advantage, and started in pursuit, and had gone no great distance when a file of Indians were seen approaching. Both parties hurried forward to secure the position of a rising ground near at hand. Standish got to it first, and the Indians at once scattered, sheltering themselves behind trees, and discharged a flight of arrows at their opponents, and then fled to the swamp; only one of the party being injured, a shot breaking his arm.

The Weston colony now dispersed, Standish supplying them with corn, and with what they had robbed the Indians of was sufficient whereon to sustain life. Standish and his party returned, carrying with them the head of Wituwamat to ornament the Plymouth Block-House, as a terror to the Indians. Three men only remained, who had straggled off to an Indian settlement, and whom the Indians put to death in retaliation.

LOVELL'S GROVE.

PINE-POINT HOTEL.

Afterward, speaking of their fate, the Indians said, "When we killed your men, they cried and made ill-favored faces." They were probably put to death with tortures, which distinguish Indian executions.

Thus in failure, disgrace, and murder, ended the first attempt of a settlement at Weymouth; and, as we sail up this beautiful river, we can hardly conceive of the terrible sufferings and deeds of violence and bloodshed perpetrated on these now peaceful-appearing shores.

On entering the river, a small rocky island will be observed on the right hand, or "starboard" as we should say when aboard ship. This is called Raccoon Island.

After a delightful sail up the river, during which many beautiful views can be obtained of the surrounding country, we arrive at Quincy Point, where a bridge crosses the river, which here forms the dividing line between Weymouth and Quincy. On the Weymouth side of the river, near the steamboat landing, is Lovell's Grove, one of the most charming pleasure resorts in the harbor. There are many handsome buildings connected with the grove, such as the dance-halls, restaurant, billiard-hall, bowling-ally, and octagon, summer, and bath houses, and many devices provided for the entertainment of the old and young, such as tilting-boards, swings, flying-horses, and many other things that our space will not permit a full description of.

Directly opposite the grove is the Pine-Point Hotel, where clam-bakes are provided daily, and where abundant refreshments of the choicest and best quality will be provided to hungry excursionists, who, while enjoying the good cheer that the house affords, can contrast their present condition with that of the starving settlers that once dwelt on this river.

CHAPTER XVII.

ROUTE FIFTH. — YACHTING TRIP DOWN THE HARBOR. — DESCRIPTION OF THE YACHTING RENDEZVOUS AT SOUTH BOSTON. — DORCHESTER BAY. — SAVIN HILL. — COMMERCIAL POINT. — NEPONSET RIVER. — SQUANTUM — MOUNT WOLLOSTON. — SETTLEMENT OF SAME BY CAPTAIN WOLOSTON. — THOMAS MORTON TAKES POSSESSION. — CALLED MERRY MOUNT. — MAY-POLE ERECTED. — DISPLEASURE OF THE PLYMOUTH PEOPLE. — STANDISH BREAKS UP THE SETTLEMENT.

The great yachting rendezvous of Boston and its vicinity is at South Boston Point, which is easily reached by horse-cars or in the summer season by the new line of steamers that ply between Foster's Wharf, City Point, and Long Island. The great attractions that are offered to yachtsmen at the Point is the depth of water, the yachts remaining afloat at all times, and a landing can be made at the different rafts at all stages of the tide. There is but little passing of vessels in Dorchester Bay, and the yachts run no danger of being run down at their moorings; and, again, the Point being the easternmost part of the main-land situated near the city, it gives the yachtsman a good start down the harbor, and, being so ready of access by means of the horse-cars, which run every few minutes, as a yachting rendezvous it cannot be surpassed by any place on the coast. There are located here the two principal Yacht Clubs of New England, — the Boston and the South-Boston Yacht Clubs. Both are incorporated associations, and have commodious houses, wharves, lockers, and so forth, and the best accommodations for yachtsmen that can be found anywhere.

Both Club Houses are located at the foot of Sixth Street, and command a fine view of the harbor and islands. The yachts of each club are moored a short distance off shore, numbering several hundred of every conceivable rig, — sloops, schooners, steamers, and a great number of cat-boats. This latter seems to be the favorite rig, as the boats

BOSTON YACHT-CLUB HOUSE.

can be easily managed, and for a few hours' sail in the bay it is the most convenient boat to have.

Beside the yacht clubs, there are numerous hotels or shore-houses, at nearly all of which yachts can be hired with competent skippers if required, each house having a wharf and float stage connected with it. Clam chowder, fish dinner, and other good things can also be procured there. The number of people visiting these establishments has been steadily increasing during the past few years. On Sundays or any holiday during the summer season, the Point is visited by immense crowds of people seeking a breath of pure sea air, and watching or participating in a " sail " on Dorchester Bay.

The vacant land that yet remains at the Point should certainly be taken by the city, and used for a public park; for there is no section of the city that offers the inducements in the warm weather that South-Boston Point does to the masses of the people that are unable to go to a longer distance into the country, and there is no more beautiful sight of a sultry day than to sit under the veranda of one of the beach-houses, and watch the yachts sailing with their snowy sails over the blue waters of the bay, bending gracefully to the freshing breeze.

Two first-class hotels are situated here, — the Atlantic House and the Point-Pleasant House, — where board can be obtained for the summer months, so that the yachtsmen and others that enjoy sailing can be near their business, and enjoy better advanatges for boating than can be obtained by going to the beach at a much farther distance from home.

This is also the only place in the city where open-sea bathing can be enjoyed. Free baths are provided for ladies and gentlemen, where bathing on the beach can be enjoyed in much warmer water than on the beaches at the entrance to the harbor.

In this chapter we purpose to lay out a sailing route which will describe different portions of the harbor not visited by the steamers. Starting from the " Point," and sailing in a southerly direction across Dorchester Bay, one of the first points of interest noticed will be Savin Hill, a high rocky hill situated on the end of a peninsula, and rising very abruptly from the water by which it is nearly surrounded. It is covered to its summit with very dense woods, mostly savin-trees, hence its name. It is mentioned in the third chapter of this work, where it is alluded to in Roger Clap's Narrative, and described as follows under the name of Rock Hill: —

SAVIN HILL: NORTHEAST VIEW.

"It seems many of these People were Trading men & at first designed Dorchester for a place of Trade and accordingly built a fort at Rock Hill wherein were several peices of ordinance near ye Waterside."

Although this was selected from the first landing of the white men for a place of settlement, yet until the last few years no houses were built on it, with the exception of one on the north side of the hill, said to have been Washington's headquarters. Recently many fine residences have been erected here; two beautiful avenues are laid out that encircle the Hill, Savin-Hill Avenue and the Grampian Way. The residences bordering these avenues contain beautifully laid-out grounds; many of them being quite extensive. The hill is rocky, and with its woods, and the magnificent view that can be obtained of the surrounding country from its summit, cannot be surpassed by any other place in the vicinity of Boston; for, although it is within three miles of the State House, and also within the city limits, and in the midst of large and finely kept estates, surrounding handsome dwelling-houses, yet by ascending the hill the reader will plunge into a wilderness, where in some instances progress is forbidden by beetling cliffs or thorny thickets, and where the forest is seen in its primitive wilderness, and as he reaches the brow of the rocky cliff that marks the summit, away off to the eastward can be seen old ocean and Nantasket's pride, her beaches, and the Brewsters, with their ragged storm-beaten shores, and to the north and west the vision gathers in the ever-enlarging metropolis and inland towns, and to the south is Quincy's beauties in rolling hills and ample plains, backed by the bold outlines of the Blue Hills, whence flows the beautiful Neponset River, entering the bay at the feet of the beholder, and the inland scenery is in lovely contrast with the ocean's broad expanse in the other distance. The view we give of Savin Hill is from the northeast, and made from a photograph.

Directly south of Savin Hill is Commercial Point, situated on the west bank of the Neponset, where it enters the harbor. It has been used from the earliest settlement of Dorchester for the purpose its name indicates, and here the Dorchester people located their wharves, on account of there being a greater depth of water here, and also its sheltered position and its situation at the entrance to the Neponset River, which has been of great importance at all periods of the history of New England, and which is about thirty miles from its source in Foxborough to Boston Harbor, and is navigable to Granite Bridge, and formerly to the Lower Mills, a distance of about four miles in a crooked course from Commercial Point. By the curious connection between the Charles River and Neponset River, by means of Mother Brook, it literally forms a large island of the territory consisting of Boston, Roxbury, West Roxbury, Dorchester, Dedham, Newton, Brighton, and Brookline, and the entire distance can be passed in a small boat, that can be carried around the several dams that intercept its course, and produce, with the neighboring scenery, picturesque falls.

This river separates Dorchester from Squantum, a place frequently mentioned in these pages, and closely connected with the history of the harbor, and the most picturesque and romantic spot in the harbor. The view we here present of that portion of it known as Squaw Rock, or, as it is called in the old records, Pulpit Rock, and often Chapel Rock, is made from a photograph, and shows a very correct view of the squaw's head or profile. Very few people living in Boston know of the natural beauties of this place, and of its attractions, or of this wonderful image of a squaw's head cut by nature in the solid rock. In fact, the summer resorts of the White Mountains and other far-off localities hundreds of miles away are better known to the average Bostonian than the superior attractions of the romantic and beautiful scenery of Boston Harbor, simply because interested parties connected with hotels, railroads, steamboats, and so forth, spend thousands of dollars every year in advertising their different lines of travel to the summer resorts at the mountains, lakes, springs, and so forth, the attractions of which are in a great measure exaggerated.

Squantum is about seven miles from Boston by road, over which a delightful drive can be had in the summer-time, and is about three miles from Long Wharf by water. The first description we have of it is in Myles Standish's account of his explorations in Boston Harbor and is supposed to have taken its name from Tisquantum, his Indian guide on that occasion, and is the place where he went ashore with his men, and marched three miles up the country, and came across an Indian Fort and village, containing only women, whom Tisquantum "would have rifled of their furs and corn, if he had not been constrained."

The shores of Squantum are rocky, with a very good showing of trees on and about the place, relieving it of the nakedness that disfigures some of the islands and headlands of the harbor. There are also some beautiful walks and drives here through the lanes and roads, and the view that can be obtained from the summit of the rocks back of the hotel cannot be surpassed from any other point in the harbor. Here the reader can see the ocean and the harbor laid out before him like a panorama; and a magnificent view of the surrounding country, including Boston, Roxbury, Dorchester, Quincy, Braintree, Weymouth, Hingham, and Cohasset can be obtained from this place of observation.

Squantum is surrounded on nearly all sides by water, and is separated from Thompson's Island by what is known as Squantum Gut; but the current is nothing like as strong as in Hull Gut or Shirley Gut. The Hotel here is kept by Mr. William Reed, a veteran in the hotel business; and a better shot for wild fowl or a better boatman cannot be found on the coast, which the writer knows by experience, having been in his company for over six months during a gunning and boating trip to Florida in the winter season, starting from Squantum in November, and returning the next May, and sailing outside off the coast during the worst months for shipwrecks in the whole year, and making the trip in the cat-boat "Crosby," 26 feet long, which may be seen at the float-stage; and, if the reader should desire a sail in the harbor at any time, there is not a safer boat or more reliable skipper than Mr. Reed.

Squantum was noted during the early part of the present century for the Squantum Feasts, held there not only by the fast young men of the time, but also by the staid and respectable old gentlemen of Boston and the neighboring towns.

Squantum would make an excellent place for summer residences, or for a suburban park, and at the present time could be purchased at an extremely low figure.

Passing through Squantum Gut, and sailing in an easterly direction by Moon Head, we enter Quincy Bay, on the south side of which will be noticed a hill covered over pretty thickly with houses. This is Mount Wollaston or Merry Mount, frequent mention of which has been made in these pages. About five years after the distrastrous attempt at settling Weymouth, Thomas Morton, one of the settlers, and described as a lawyer of Furnival's Inn, London, persuaded Captain Woloston and three or four partners to settle at this place, which is but a short distance from Wessagusset. In September, 1625, Captain Woloston, with thirty adventurers, landed here, and began a plantation near where the house of John Quincy Adams now stands. During the absence of Captain Woloston to Virginia on a trading voyage, Morton instigated the settlers to rebel against Lieutenant Filcher, who was left in command, and choose him in his stead.

From this time dates all the future troubles of this place, of which so much has been said. Morton commenced his free-and-easy reign by setting up a May-pole, and christening the place Merry Mount, which was a lamentable spectacle to the Puritans at Plymouth. They called it an idol, — yea, they called it the Calf of Horeb, — and stood at defiance with the place, and called it Mount Dagon, and threatened to make it a woeful Mount, and not a Merry Mount. Having no cares, they gave themselves up to a gay and hilarious system of living, drinking and dancing around the May-pole adorned on the top with a buck's horns, like so many faries or furies, as if they had revived the celebrated feasts of the Roman goddess, Flora, or the mad practices of the Bacchanalians. Morton described the naming of the place as follows: —

"And being resolved to have the new name confirmed for a memorial to after ages did devise to have it performed in solemn Revels and merriment after the old English custom and therefore brewed a barrel of excellent beare and provided a case of bottles to be spent in good cheer, for all comers of that day, and because they would make a complete thing of it they prepared a song for the occasion. And upon May-day they brought the May-pole to the place appointed with drums, gunnes, pistols, and other fitting instruments for that purpose and there erected it with the help of the Salvages that came there a purpose to see the manner of our Revels. A goodly pine tree of eighty foot was reared up, with a pair of buckshorns nayled one somewheare near the top of it, where it stood as a faire sea mark for directions how to find out the way to mine host of Ma-re-Mount. And we had a poem in readiness made which was fixed to the May-pole to shew the new name confirmed on the plantation. And this harmless mirth was much distasteful to the Puritans, and from that time sought occasion against my honest Host of Ma-re-Mount to overthrow his undertakings and to destroy his plantation quite and clean."

They were joined in their revels by the Indians; for Morton, by his kind treatment of them, secured their lasting friendship, they keeping him and the rest of the company supplied with game, thus showing how susceptible the Indians were to kind treatment. And this was another grievance to the Plymouth people, that they should be on social terms with the savages; for by this they secured the trade in beaver-skins, and held very questionable relations with the Indian women, and there were fears of there being a mixed population soon.

After fruitless efforts at reform, through written admonishments which the carnal Morton received in a most unsatisfactory spirit of contumely, the Pilgrim fathers of Plymouth despatched the redoubtable Myles Standish (who seems to have been a sort of border ruffian of his day) to the scene of trouble to set matters right the same as he did five years before when he murdered the Indians so treacherously at Weymouth. The following is what Standish says of the affair: —

"So they resolved to take Morton by force. Which was accordingly done; but they found him stand stifly in his defence having made fast his dors, armed his consorts, set divers dishes of powder and bullits ready on ye table and if they had not been over armed with drink, more hurt might have been done. They somaned him to yeeld, but he kept his house, and they could get nothing but scofes & scorns from him; but at length fearing they would do some violence to ye house, he and some of his crue came out, but not yeeld, but to shoote; but they were so steeld with drinks as their peeces were too heavie for them; him self with a carbine (over charged & allmost halfe fild with powder & shote as was after found) had thought to have shot Captain Standish, but he stept to him & put by his piece & took him. Neither was ther any hurt done either side save yt one was so drunk yt he ran his own nose upon ye pointe of a sword yt one held before him as he entered yt house, but he lost but a little of his hott blood."

The accounts of this affair widely differ. The following is Morton's description of it: —

"Now Captain Shrimp (Morton's nickname for Standish) takes eight persons more to him and they imbarque with preparations against Ma-re Mount. Now the nine Worthies are approached; and mine Host (Morton) prepared, having intelligence by a Salvage that hastened in love from Wessagusset to give him notice of their intent. The nine Worthies comming before the Denne of this supposed monster, this seven headed hydra, as they termed him, and began to offer quarter if mine host (Morton) would yield, had the rest not bin from home, we would have given Capt. Shrimp, (a quondam Drummer), such a well-come as would have made him wish for a Drume as bigg as Diogenes' tubb that hee might have crept into it ought of sight. Yet to save the effusion of so much worthy bloud as would have issued out of the vaynes of these 9 worthies of New Canaan if mine Host should have played upon them out of his port holes, for they came within danger like a flock of wild geese, as if they had bin tayled one to another as coults to be sold at a faier, mine host was content to yeeld upon quarter, and did capitulate with them, but mine Host had no sooner set open the dore and issued out, but instantly Captain Shrimp and the rest of the worthies stepped to him, layd hold of his armes, and had him downe and so eagerly was every man bent against him, not regarding any agreement made with such a carnal man that they fell upon him, as if they would have eaten him up. Captain Shrimp by this outrageous riot thus made himself master of mine Host of Ma-re Mount and disposed of what hee had at his plantation."

Morton says that the conspirators "feasted their bodies and fell to tippeling as if they had obtained a great prize," in precisely the same manner as the state constables would do at the present day.

A writer, describing Boston seventy years after the Merry-Mount affair, shows that the inhabitants here had not changed their ways during that period. He describes the place and people as follows :—

"Every Stranger is forced to take notice that in Boston there is more

Religious Zelots than Honest men, more Parsons than Churches. That the people are very busy at detecting one another's failings, and he is accounted by their Church Governor a Meretorious Christian that betrays his Neighbor to a Whipping-post."

And such cases of injustice and intolerance even prevail in this State to the present day; a case of which came to the writer's notice but recently, in an English paper, written by a tourist in Boston, who stated that while stopping at the Parker House, having some leisure time to spare he went across the street to the Court House, and was very much astonished to see hotel keepers and others fined or sent to prison for selling liquor, and was still further astonished, on returning to the hotel to dinner, to see some of the very judges at the bar drinking liquor, thus aiding and abetting the very crime which they had just sentenced men for committing. This of course must have occurred during the enforcement of the prohibitory law a few years ago, and shows that we have yet considerable of the old Puritanical spirit of intolerance that hung the Quakers and other unbelievers, and burnt the witches, and massacred the Indians.

CHAPTER XVIII.

WEYMOUTH BACK RIVER. — DELIGHTFUL CAMPING PLACE. — DESCRIPTION OF SLATE ISLAND. — THE GREAT BREWSTER. — DESCRIPTION OF THE LIGHT-HOUSE. — IS DESTROYED BY THE BRITISH. — REBUILT IN 1783. — MIDDLE BREWSTER. — OUTER BREWSTER. — ITS ROMANTIC APPEARANCE. — CALF AND GREEN ISLAND. — THE GRAVES. — MANY WRECKS OCCUR ON THESE ISLANDS YEARLY. — MINOT'S-LEDGE LIGHT. — ITS DESTRUCTION IN THE GREAT STORM OF 1851. — REBUILT IN 1860.

Sailing in a southeasterly direction between Pettick's Island and Hough's Neck, past the entrance to the Weymouth Fore River, and between Grape Island and Lower Neck, we enter Weymouth Back River, one of the most delightful camping places in the harbor. The easterly shore is well wooded, and the land is high and rocky. There is some beautiful scenery up the river, many parts of the shore being wooded to the water's edge, presenting a very picturesque and romantic appearance.

The river can be ascended as far up as the falls at East Weymouth, and the sail or row up the river will amply repay the yachtsman for his trouble. Leaving Back River, and sailing in a northerly direction between Grape Island and Slate Island, we leave the latter on the starboard. This island is composed of slate-stones, whence its name, and is covered with a dense thicket of elderberry and bayberry bushes. Quantities of slate have been obtained from this island years ago; and, although the material has not been of a remarkable quality for the protection of roofs, it has done good service for underpinning and for cellar walls.

Lately a considerable part of the island has been taken away for ballast, which ought to be stopped, for at the present rate of destruction nothing will be left of the island in a few years but a shoal.

BOSTON LIGHT.

Continuing on through Hull Gut, we soon come to the main ship-channel, lying between the promontory on the south, on which is situated the town of Hull, and the cluster of islands and rocks on the north known as the Brewsters, on one of which is situated "Boston Light."

Having described somewhat fully the islands of the harbor, and the various passages around and among them, as well as the numerous small coves or harbors connected therewith, before closing this work we will say a few words about this singular group of islands lying at the entrance to the harbor. The first of these, as the harbor is left, is the Great Brewster, which contains about twenty-five acres of land, a great bluff very imperfectly protected by a sea-wall being very prominent on its "Southerly Point," so called. The island was bought in 1848 by the City of Boston of Mr. Lemuel Brackett, and a portion ceded to the United States the following year for the purpose of building a sea-wall for the better protection of the harbor, the channels of which were rapidly shoaling from the washing-away of this island, the *débris* of which formed a spit extending westerly a mile and a half long, which is dry at low tide, and upon the extremity of which is the Beacon, or Bug Light, mentioned in a previous chapter. The cottage seen on the island is the summer residence of the Hon. Benjamin Dean, who leased the island from the city.

Southeast of the Great Brewster, and connected with it by a bar which is exposed at low water, is the Little Brewster, on which is situated the chief light-house of the harbor.

The inhabitants of Boston began very early in the last century to consider the subject of establishing a light-house at the entrance to the harbor, so large had become their commerce with foreign countries. Accordingly in 1715 an act was passed, " to build a light-house on the southernmost point of the Great Brewster called Beacon Island, because there had been a great discouragement to navigation by the loss of the lives and estates of several of His Majesties subjects, and that after the building of the light-house and kindling a light, in it to be kept from sun setting to sun rising, that an impost shall be paid by the masters of all Ships and Vessels, coming in and going out of the harbor. Except

Coasters the duty of One Peny per Ton, Inwards and One Peny per Ton, Outwards, before they Load or Unload the Goods therein."

The first light-house keeper was George Worthylake, who was brought up in the harbor, and whose father had been for many years a resident of the island where Fort Warren is now situated. He himself dwelt at Lovell's Island, where his farm was. He was paid fifty pounds for his services the first year, but had an increase the second year to seventy pounds on account of the loss of fifty-nine sheep which were drowned during the winter of 1716, they having been driven into the sea by a storm through want of his care of them when obliged to attend the light-house. Mr. Worthylake was unfortunately drowned, together with his wife Ann and his daughter Ruth, off Noddle's Island, now East Boston, while on their way to the town. This incident was the origin of the ballad called the "Light-house Tragedy," which Franklin says he was induced by his brother to write, print, and sell about the street, and which he says sold prodigiously, though it was " wretched stuff."

The old light-house was much injured by fire in 1751, and was struck several times by lightning. During the Revolutionary War it fared hard. A party went from Milton in 1775, and destroyed all its wood work and the lantern; and, after it had been repaired by the British Admiral Graves, it was destroyed again the same year. After the British evacuated Boston the Continentals began to bring their guns to bear on the fleet, and Mr. Ezekiel Price narrates that " about six o'clock June 13, 1776, the cannon on Long Island began to play upon the shipping, which obliged them to weigh their anchors, and make the best of their way out of the harbor. As they passed Nantasket and the light-house our artillery gave them some shot from Nantasket Hill." [The earthworks can still be seen near the signal station at Hull.] "The enemy sent their boats on shore at Light-house Island and brought from thence a party there placed of Regulars, afterward which they destroyed the

Light-house, and then the whole fleet made all the sail they could and went to sea steering their course eastward."

The commander of this ship, the " Renown," of fifty guns, Captain Bangs, after taking off his men from the island, left a quantity of gunpowder so arranged that it took fire about an hour afterward, and blew up the brick tower.

The present light-house was erected in 1783, but has been several times refitted since then with improved apparatus, and in 1860 the old tower was raised in height, it now measuring ninety-eight feet above sea-level. The white tower with its black lantern and revolving light can be seen at a distance of sixteen nautical miles if the weather be fair and the sky clear, and is an imposing object with its neighbor the foghorn when viewed from vessels on entering or leaving the harbor.

Northeast of the Great Brewster is the Middle Brewster, composed almost entirely of rocks, but it has upon it about ten acres of fair soil fit for cultivation. This island has several neatly constructed houses on it, in which reside the families of fishermen and other seafaring men, and on the top of the island will be noticed a handsome square cottage, which is the summer residence of Augustus Russ, Esq. Farther east lies the Outer Brewster, apparently a huge mass of rocks cut up by the sea into ravines and chasms; yet within this rough exterior is contained an oasis of good soil and a natural pond and spring of fresh water. A small house stood in this fertile spot a few years ago, inhabited for a number of years by the late Mr. Austin, who owned the island, and led a hermit's life here for many years. He made an artificial harbor hewed out of the solid rock, which nearly divides it into two islands. This was intended for a haven for small vessels, and with a gate at its mouth it furnished a good dock when occasion required. The owners of this property at one time expected to realize considerable by the sale of stone for building purposes. But now Mr. Austin is dead, the house burnt by roughs from the city, and the harbor destroyed by storms which have made such inroads of late years as to separate the island into two parts in stormy weather.

This island is one of the most romantic places near Boston, far surpassing Nahant or any other place on the coast of Massachusetts Bay in

AUSTIN'S HARBOR, OUTER BREWSTER.

its wild rocks, chasms, caves, and overhanging cliffs, and is the only island in the harbor where a landing cannot be made in all weather. During a storm the island is entirely unapproachable, and many lives have been lost in trying to land in stormy weather. There is also no anchorage for a boat or vessel here at such times, and woe be to the vessel that should be driven on here in a storm, for she would go to pieces as soon as she struck, and no living soul could land on these rocks at such a time without being dashed to pieces.

The writer was on this island a short time ago, and saw the remains of

THE GORGE, OUTER BREWSTER.

a coasting schooner strewed round about the rocks, and was informed by some fishermen on the Middle Brewster that she came on the rocks during a stormy night a few months previous. They discovered in the morning her masts on the rocks, and her anchor and chains, which she had let go, but too late to save her from going on the rock and being dashed to pieces. Nothing was known as to what vessel it was, where from, or how many composed her crew. Every living being was lost. This occurs every year, and many are the vessels that have been dashed to atoms on the rocks of this island.

The island is now owned by the Hon. Benjamin Dean, who bought it of Austin's heirs a few years since for $1,000. It can hardly ever be put to any use on account of its unapproachable condition. As its name signifies, it is the outermost island in the harbor, extending beyond all others into the ocean.

South of the Outer Brewster lie the Shag Rocks. These are dangerous to mariners, and cause shipwrecks every year. In 1860 the "Maritana" was lost here, and twenty-six men perished; and only a few months ago a Philadelphia collier was lost on these rocks, which furnished the Hull wreckers with their winter supply of coal. These rocks are nearly covered at high water. The frequent loss of vessels on these rocks should be sufficient warning to the United-States authorities to proceed at once to the erection of some suitable protection against such dreadful losses.

As the Brewsters form the northern boundary to the harbor, so Point Allerton forms the southern. This point takes its name from Mr. Isaac Allerton, the famous agent of the Plymouth Company, and a passenger in the "May Flower" in 1620, and was so named by the Plymouth Pilgrims in one of their early visits here; and they called the islands at the entrance to the harbor "the Brewsters" in respect to his wife's brother and sister, the children of Mr. William Brewster, the ruling elder of New Plymouth.

North of the Great Brewster is Calf Island, containing ten acres and several houses. On this island is a very pretty grove of wild-cherry trees, some pleasant beaches, and wild basaltic rock. North of it is the Little Calf, so called, which is uninhabited.

Just north of the above-mentioned group is the Hypocrite Channel, a very dangerous passage, but little used at the present time, but in former years considered one of the principal entrances to the harbor. Through this channel we will sail on our return to the harbor, leaving on our starboard Greene Island, the least pleasantly situated of all the islands at the entrance of the harbor, yet it is not uninhabited, and at the time of the destruction of Minot's-Ledge Light in 1851, the tide rose so high that its two inhabitants had to be taken off in one of the pilot boats.

On this island resided many years a strange being, singular in his habits, and possessing a very independent spirit. Mr. Choate was not far from seventy years of age when he was forced to leave his chosen abode of twenty years, in the winter of 1865, and accept the protection of the Harbor Police. It seems in his younger days he was an ordinary seaman, and about the year 1845 he built himself a rudely constructed hut on this island, and sustained himself by fishing, subsisting on fish, lobsters, and muscles. The severity of the weather was such that he must have perished but for his timely rescue. He was sent to the almshouse at Bridgewater, where he subsequently died.

Northwest of Greene and Calf Islands are Alderidge's Ledge, Half-Tide Rocks, the Devil's Back (dry at low water), Maffit's Ledge, Commissioner's Ledge, and Barrel Rock. This last rock was a great obstruction to navigation, and was entirely removed in 1869. It was an immense boulder of Medford granite, and was undoubtedly carried there by some ancient glacier.

To the eastward are Martin's Ledge, Boston Ledge, and Roaring Bulls; and to the southeast are Thieves' Ledge (a noted fishing ground), and Harding's Ledge, the most dangerous obstacles to the entrance to the harbor, on which many vessels are lost. A few years ago a steamer went to pieces on these rocks. The Big Harding is four feet out of water at low tide. On this ledge is placed a bell-buoy and beacon.

Northeast of the Brewsters is the Graves, on which there is a horn-buoy, whose dismal notes can be heard at all times, caused by the rising and falling of the sea, which forces the air through the horn, making a

THE GRAVES.

most mournful sound, like a funeral dirge for the many deaths that have occurred on its treacherous rocks, so truly and fearfully named, for they have too often proved to be the graves of the sea-tossed and worn-out mariner when in sight of his home and friends, after supposing all trials and dangers were passed. A landing on these rocks can be made only when the sea is smooth. In storms they are completely washed, and the surf breaks over the highest part of them.

Six miles southeast of the Hardings is Minot's-Ledge Light, built on the extreme end of the ledge, which extends out about two miles into the ocean from the Cohasset shore, and is the most dangerously situated light-house on the Atlantic coast, rising as it does from the waters to a great height, and in rough weather the sea breaks completely over it, swaying the solid tower of rock violently to and fro, so that a bucket of water slops over, leaving it only about half full. The foundation is beneath the water, and is partially artificial, as there was not sufficient rock there to build the light-house on without adding to it. During the great storm of April 16, 1851, the light-house was destroyed, and the keepers lost their lives. The foundation stone of the present tower was laid in 1858, and the light-house completed in 1860.

Returning to the harbor by way of the Hypocrite Channel, Broad Sound and President's Roads, as marked on the map with dotted lines, we arrive back again at City Point, our place of departure; and with this chapter the description of the islands and harbor closes.

www.ingramcontent.com/pod-product-compliance
Lightning Source LLC
Chambersburg PA
CBHW020116170426
43199CB00009B/550